A SURVEY OF
VANDALISM
TO ARCHAEOLOGICAL
RESOURCES

IN SOUTHWESTERN
COLORADO

Paul R. Nickens

Signa L. Larralde

Gordon C. Tucker, Jr.

BUREAU OF
LAND MANAGEMENT
COLORADO

**CULTURAL
RESOURCES
SERIES**

Number 11

FOREWORD

This study of vandalism to archaeological resources represents a new management approach by the Bureau of Land Management in protecting our cultural heritage. The study was originally done by Nickens and Associates of Montrose under a contract (YA-512-CT9-205) to the BLM. The intent of the work was to use different sources of information such as data on known vandalized sites and interviews with former or current artifact collectors to determine the source, type, and extent of the vandalism problem in southwestern Colorado.

The result of this study has allowed the BLM to make better and more productive use of its limited protection funds. Our protection effort is now emphasizing three areas: public education on the heritage value of cultural resources, interpretation and stabilization of the more visible and important resources, and the use of patrol and law enforcement to deter vandals from further destruction of these non-renewable heritage values.

It is my pleasure to present this latest volume of the Cultural Resource Series to the public and to the professional community. It is also my pleasure to note that this study has been put into practical operation in southwestern Colorado in our continuing effort to protect and enhance our rich cultural heritage of that area of Colorado.

GEORGE FRANCIS
State Director, Colorado
Bureau of Land Management
July, 1981

PREFACE

This report has been prepared in partial fulfillment of Bureau of Land Management Contract YA-512-CT9-205, entitled, "A Study of Access and Other Factors Affecting Vandalism to Archaeological Sites in Southwestern Colorado." A previously submitted report, also required under terms of the contract, provided an overview of the archaeological resources on BLM lands in southwestern Colorado (Nickens 1980). The present volume examines the ongoing problem of vandalism to cultural resource sites in the Sacred Mountain Planning Unit, which comprises a large portion of the San Juan Resource Area of the BLM Montrose District.

In addition to the junior authors, many persons have made important contributions toward the completion of this study. From our office this includes Susan M. Chandler, Alan D. Reed, Janet R. Sprouse, and Susan O'Connell. Continuous support and assistance was provided by BLM archaeologists associated with the project area, including Dr. Douglas D. Scott, District Archaeologist, Gary Matlock and Kristy Arrington of the San Juan Resource Area office, and Steve Fuller, Supervisory Archaeologist, BLM Dolores. The efforts of each of these men and women are greatly appreciated.

Special gratitude is due Fred Blackburn for his efforts to compile and tabulate data relating to vandalism from the BLM site files, and for sharing his insight on various aspects of the overall problem. For providing numerous forms of information and comments, we thank Dr. Bruce Rippeteau, then the State Archaeologist, John Deans, BLM Colorado State Office, Peter Pilles, Forest Archaeologist, Coconino National Forest in Arizona, Max Witkind, Army Corps of Engineers, Arkansas, archaeologists with the Dolores Project, Ed and Jo Berger, Crow Canyon School, Cortez, and the Montezuma County Sheriff's Department.

Finally, we would like to express appreciation to the thirty anonymous local informants who shared their views and thoughts concerning vandalism and protection of cultural resources in the study area. The usefulness of this information is readily evident in the report.

Paul R. Nickens
Principal Investigator

TABLE OF CONTENTS

LIST OF FIGURES

Page

Figure No.

LIST OF TABLES

ABSTRACT

One of the most critical concerns for land managers and professional archaeologists is vandalism or unwarranted destruction of vestiges of the nation's historic and prehistoric cultural resources. Though illegal since 1906, the attrition of archaeological sites and data on public lands has been and continues to be a serious problem. This study undertakes analysis of the factors affecting vandalism to archaeological sites in the Bureau of Land Management's Sacred Mountain Planning Unit, located in southwestern Colorado. The study area has long been known for its many spectacular prehistoric ruins and, as a consequence, relic or artifact collecting has been a common pastime since the 1880s.

In order to define factors associated with vandalism from which recommendations for improved management and conservation of the area's ruins could be made, several phases of inquiry were outlined. These include: 1) a review of activities which are deleterious to cultural resources; 2) an overview of cultural resource destruction in the project area; 3) a compilation of known site data through the use of certain variables thought to be important to the problem; 4) a field implementation phase designed to verify the trends and factors identified in the known site file data; and 5) interviews with known collectors of antiquities living in the area. As a result of these efforts, quantitative data are offered to support previous ideas that in the project area archaeological site density, distribution, and visibility, along with relatively easy access, are the principal factors associated with vandalism to cultural resources. Other factors of secondary importance include the local and family traditions of artifact collecting, and a commercial or profit motive. Recommendations to management center on actions related to the need for demonstrable intent to prosecute violators of extant antiquities laws, expansion of existing preventative programs, and continued and increased emphasis on public education approaches.

INTRODUCTION

General

The Bureau of Land Management (BLM) is required to identify, evaluate, and protect historic and prehistoric cultural resources on public lands under its jurisdiction. This requirement to ensure that Bureau-initiated or Bureau-authorized actions do not inadvertently harm or destroy cultural resources is mandated by various pieces of legislation, including: the Antiquities Act of 1906 (34 Stat. 224); the National Historic Preservation Act of 1966 (80 Stat. 915), as amended in 1976; the National Environmental Policy Act of 1969 (83 Stat. 852); Executive Order 11593; and the Archaeological Resources Protection Act of 1979 (P.L. 96-95).

One of the more difficult and ongoing management problems relating to cultural resources involves the protection of archaeological sites from the destructive activities of human vandals who take advantage of the accessibility which characterizes public lands to loot and plunder the nation's cultural heritage. The problem is compounded in areas which have an exceptionally significant, diverse, and abundant archaeological resource base. In such areas manpower and fiscal constraints often lead to general difficulties in fulfilling responsibilities to protect and conserve the resources. Further, it must be recognized that the problem is not a simple one; many factors are involved in understanding why vandalism occurs and even more arise to complicate the situation when solutions are sought to help eradicate such activities.

The following document is intended to provide background information concerning the extent of human vandalism to cultural resources located on BLM lands in southwestern Colorado. It is hoped that by reviewing the overall problem, a range of viable recommendations may be offered which will aid the BLM in making management decisions regarding amelioration of archaeological site vandalism.

Characteristics of the Project Area

The public lands under consideration are located in Montezuma
and Dolores Counties, southwestern Colorado. The project area, designated as the Sacred Mountain Planning Unit, is part of the BLM San Juan
Resource Area, Montrose District. Some 702,000 total acres are included
within the boundaries of the planning unit (Fig. 1), of which approximately 217,000 acres are managed by the BLM.

Recent contracted efforts have resulted in extensive documentation
of the environmental and cultural resource characteristics found in the
area. These include a class II, sample-oriented archaeological inventory which resulted in a predictive cultural resource site model for
various environmental zones within the planning unit (Chandler, Reed,
and Nickens 1980). A second report, completed under the same contract
calling for the present document, undertook a comprehensive overview of
cultural resources for the entire San Juan Resource Area (Nickens 1980).
The availability of these two reports dictates that a thorough delineation of the cultural resource background is not necessary herein;
however, a brief review follows to provide introduction to the report.
Readers desiring a more detailed description of the highly significant
cultural resources found in the Sacred Mountain Planning Unit are
encouraged to consult the sources cited above.

At the present, there are nearly 8000 archaeological sites which
have been formally recorded by archaeologists in Montezuma and Dolores
Counties. Of this total, about 3500 have been recorded on BLM lands
in the Sacred Mountain Planning Unit. These figures represent only a
fraction of the actual number of sites. Based on the class II planning
unit inventory, it has been estimated that some 7000 sites may be
located on public lands in the planning unit, with an average density
of 22.6 sites per square mile (Chandler, Reed, and Nickens 1980:112).

By far the largest number of these sites is associated with the
prehistoric Anasazi occupation of the entire Four Corners region between
ca. A.D. 1 and 1300. Sites dating to earlier culture periods in North
American prehistory, the Paleo-Indian big game hunters and the Archaic

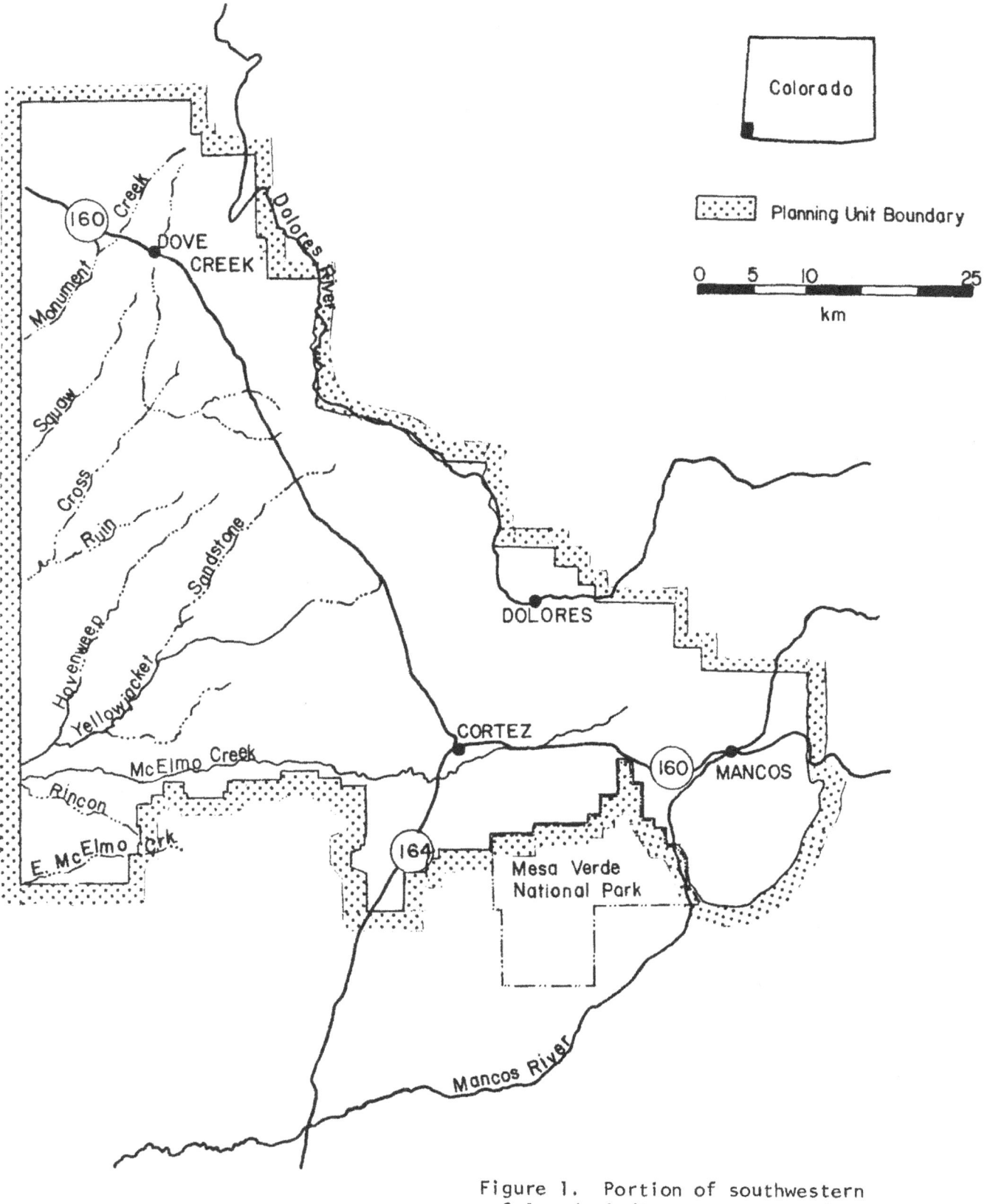

Figure 1. Portion of southwestern Colorado indicating the boundaries of the Sacred Mountain Planning Unit, major towns and highways.

3

hunter-collectors, are rare in southwestern Colorado. Similarly, sites from cultural groups who followed the Anasazi, including the proto-historic - historic Navajo and Ute are also uncommon in the project area. Even cultural resource sites associated with Euro-American settlement of southwestern Colorado are infrequently recorded in comparison to Anasazi sites. As a consequence of this uneven distribution, all documentation currently on hand regarding vandalism of archaeological resources relates to resources dated to the Anasazi occupation.

The early Anasazi are categorized as "basketmakers," reflective of a lack of ceramic containers. During the initial periods of the Anasazi sequence--Basketmaker II (A.D. 1-500) and Basketmaker III (A.D. 500-750)--the aboriginal groups were in the process of shifting away from a previous subsistence of hunting and collecting of wild plants and animals to one based on the cultivation of domesticated crops. Along with the subsistence changeover were concomitant changes in settlement patterns, beginning in the Basketmaker periods and continuing in the three sequent Pueblo periods: Pueblo I (A.D. 750-900), Pueblo II (A.D. 900-1100), and Pueblo III (A.D. 1100-1300).

One of the more important of these changes, at least for site types in the present project area, was a trend toward more sedentary and nucleated communities. At first semi-subterranean pithouse domiciliary units served this function, but in Pueblo I times villages of surface rectangular living and storage rooms became popular, and true masonry developed. By the Pueblo II era a fairly uniform village layout had been adopted. Each community evinced a roomblock, usually constructed of masonry, with a subterranean religious chamber, the kiva, located to the south. Farther south of the kiva was the village midden, or trash area, often a favorite interment place for the dead as well. While this form of village layout was not universal during the period, it was the most prevalent Pueblo II site type in southwestern Colorado.

The Pueblo III period witnessed even larger population aggregates that constructed large, open pueblos and, in some areas, the cliff dwellings with which the late Anasazi are most often identified. Still the use of the kiva and the presence of midden-burial grounds continued. Other significant site types of the Pueblo periods include the distinctive tower structures and water-control systems.

By A.D. 1300, the Anasazi had withdrawn from the Four Corners Region, leaving behind thousands of abandoned villages which had been constructed over the span of fourteen centuries. It is these vestiges of the Anasazi way of life which form a major part of the area's cultural resource base and hunting grounds for vandals and looters.

Project Goals

The primary goal of our work is to provide the BLM with data important to understanding of factors affecting human vandalism of archaeological sites in the Sacred Mountain Planning Unit. Included in this aim is the attempt to develop an objective estimate of the nature and type of vandalism occurring at the sites, and to make recommendations to the BLM to assist in the protective management of the resource base.

A second goal is to present quantitative data on which to evaluate the overall problem. Despite an accruing amount of literature on the subject of archaeological site vandalism, few "hard facts" are available concerning incidence and nature of vandalism.

Third, we wish to present not only the archaeologist's and land manager's point of view, but the perspective of the artifact collector as well. This widely-used technique in cultural anthropology attempts to gain insight into the "participant's" views on a subject since it often differs radically from the "outsider's" perspective. In this case, the participants are the collectors and the outsiders are represented by the archaeological profession and land managers. We feel this approach is important to solving the problem of widespread vandalism since virtually all the available information is biased toward the outsiders.

Methods

In order to fulfill the project goals, several phases of inquiry were designated to collect the desired data. Each of these phases is briefly listed below; more detailed explanations are contained at appropriate points in the following chapters.

1. Initially, a thorough literature review was undertaken for the purpose of identifying sources pertaining to past and present vandalism to cultural resources. In that vandalistic activities were known to have a fairly long history in southwestern Colorado, nearly coincident with the span of White settlement, we thought it important to trace the history of vandalism and to identify historical factors related to the problem.

2. Since this report undertakes discussion of only one type of several possible modes of destruction which result in the loss of archaeological data, an outline of cultural resource destruction was derived to place the intentional activities of vandals in their proper context.

3. In order to make use of existing site inventory data, a set of variables felt to be critical to understanding the factors affecting vandalism was derived. Data pertaining to these variables were then extracted or measured from the archaeological site and map files at the BLM Montrose District Office. Once recorded, these data were then compared to information gained from a similar analysis of sites recorded as part of the recent class II inventory of the planning unit.

4. A sample of sites, each originally recorded as being unvandalized, was selected from the BLM site file for revisitation. The purposes of this field implementation phase were threefold: 1) to determine the amount and type of site vandalism which might have taken place since the recording of the site; 2) to field test a method of collecting important data related to vandalism which can be utilized in future studies; and 3) to provide additional primary data which could be tested against results from the critical variables noted in No. 3 above.

5. A series of interviews was undertaken with persons known to be artifact collectors in the area. To ensure collection of comparable information, a lengthy questionnaire was completed at the time of the interview.

Organization of the Report

All in all, we believe that each of the methodologies listed above resulted in important data which are critical to gaining a better understanding of archaeological site vandalism in the Sacred Mountain Planning Unit. Each yielded unique data in its own way and yet a combination of data from the various methods contributes toward a comprehensive view of the nature and type of vandalism occurring in the area today. From the combined data, it is possible to present recommendations to assure that proper protection measures are taken to minimize the future effects of vandalism to the planning unit's cultural values.

In this context, Chapter II reviews the outline of cultural resource destruction; illustrations of destructive actions, particularly examples of intentional human vandalistic acts, are included to portray the harmful effects of such actions. Next, Chapter III presents an historical overview of archaeological vandalism in southwestern Colorado, thereby establishing such practices as a local cultural tradition. Discussion of recent protection, legislative and otherwise, concludes this chapter.

Chapters IV and V contain the results of the various known site data analyses, field implementation, and informant interviews. Following presentation of this information, recommendations are made that may help reduce vandalism to cultural resources in the future. The appendices include various kinds of primary site data from the field implementation phase, a recommended format for collecting vandalism information, an example of the interview questionnaire, and verbatim opinions given by interviewees concerning managing and protecting cultural resources on public lands.

II

THE DESTRUCTION OF CULTURAL
RESOURCE SITES AND DATA

General

As noted in the previous chapter, the primary intent of this
effort is to address the problem of vandalism to cultural resource
sites in the BLM Sacred Mountain Planning Unit. As a prelude to this
analysis, however, we believe it beneficial to briefly review in toto
the various mechanisms by which the loss of cultural resource information takes place. These causal factors include both natural (or environmental) and human means. A delineation of these critical
destructive agents allows for a realization of the ever present danger
to these fragile resources, and it further places acts of vandalism in
their proper context within the wider scheme of cultural resource
destruction.

Extended discussion of the many means by which irretrievable
loss of prehistoric and historic data takes place is not our goal
herein. Rather, we intend to introduce the categories, concisely
define them, and cite some of the pertinent literature to which interested readers may refer for more detailed information. A somewhat
expanded account is presented, however, for those categories of intentional, destructive and/or vandalistic activities which originate from
human actions.

Archaeological Sites as Resources

Prior to undertaking a review of agents which lead to destruction
of cultural resources, some comments on the designation of prehistoric
and historic sites as resources is in order. Historically, archaeological sites have of course been of great concern to the professionals
who studied the remains and lifeways of former human communities, and
many of the larger, important prehistoric and historic sites were of
interest to laymen. Coincident with the realization in the past few

decades that our cultural resources constitute a finite entity has been an awareness that vestiges of our cultural heritage are being methodically destroyed, quite often at an alarming rate. The increasing demands upon our natural resources and the evergrowing use of land surface, especially in the Western states, has prompted increased concern for the archaeological sites that remain.

The concern for preservation of such resources lies in the fact that archaeological remains are defined by one group of professionals as "a limited, fragile, non-renewable part of the environment, and disturbance of them results in irreversible and cumulative impacts" (Scovill, Gordon, and Anderson 1972). In a later paper, these same authors concisely discuss the characteristics and importance of archaeological resources in the following manner:

> The investigation of the archaeological record of the American continent is the serious and scientific study of humankind over a span of time numbered in the tens of thousands of years. The study seeks knowledge--knowledge to describe, to explain, and to understand the behavior of past peoples and their interactions as integral parts of changing cultural and natural systems. Cultural history, cultural physiography, cultural ecology, and cultural processes are the current emphasis in the anthropological study of the human past through the archaeological record.

> Archaeological resources predominantly consist of the physical evidences, or cultural debris, left on the landscape by past societies. They include a wide range of these cultural debris: architectural features; tools of stone, ceramic, or wood; trash dumps; campsites, villages, or towns; the often subtle remains of plants and animals exploited for food; and the interred remains of the people themselves. Of high significance to the investigation, analysis, and interpretation of cultural debris are the local and regional geomorphological sequences, soil composition, and modern biological and botanical baseline indicators. Critically essential to the methodologies, techniques, and processes of studying archaeological resources is the preservation of the undisturbed stratigraphic context of the cultural debris. Directly stated, the cultural debris of this nation's archaeological resources have no value and are of no potential for studying the past once they have been rearranged on the landscape by a bulldozer or a dragline (Scovill, Gordon, and Anderson 1977:44).

These two paragraphs written by Scovill and his co-authors clearly convey the professional feeling regarding archaeological sites as significant resources and the reasons why protection and preservation of these resources is of consequence to those charged with management of the nation's public lands. Interested readers are also referred to William Lipe's cogent discussion on the overwhelming need for discretion on the part of today's professionals in order that meaningful portions of the overall resource are conserved for investigations of the future (Lipe 1977).

An Outline of Cultural Resource Destruction

A number of agents may be identified which, in most instances, result in damage, alteration, or loss to cultural resource sites and data when the two come into conflict. A listing of these destructive agents is shown in Figure 2, and each category is discussed in the following paragraphs. To be sure, additional agents could be readily identified and added to the list; however, we believe the categories presented cover the major factors, particularly those having deleterious effects to cultural resources in the region under discussion.

Before discussing these categories, it would be well to note several generalizations which are implicit to the outline. The first, and perhaps most obvious, fact is that a large degree of synergism exists between the agents and modes of resource destruction given in the outline. That is to say, much relationship with respect to cause and effect circumstances is clearly evident among the various categories. For example, in some cases recreation on public lands and hobby collecting (or even malicious vandalism) may be considered as related activities. On the other hand, the two may be clearly differentiated in certain instances. Likewise, a combination of erosion forces and land reclamation activities may create an ecological battlefield with cultural resources being caught in the middle.

It would be unfair, however, to wholly classify the agents listed as being inherently harmful to cultural resources. A few examples will suffice to clarify this point. Many important archaeological sites would probably go unrecognized and not be investigated were it not for the forces of natural erosion or the result of human-caused

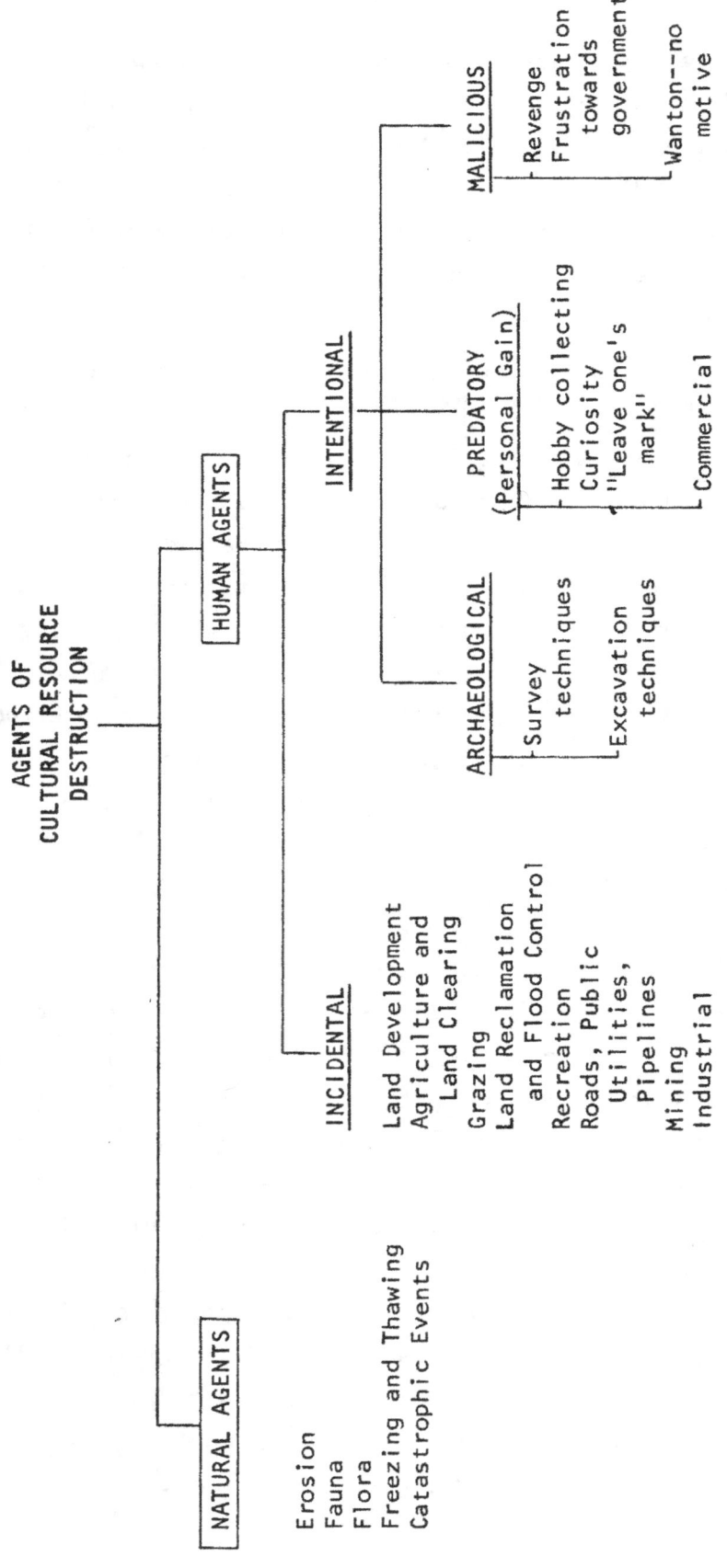

Figure 2. Outline of processes responsible for destruction of cultural resource sites and data.

12

land alteration activities, or even the efforts of interested hobbyist collectors. And we must remember that many of these agents, particularly the incidental human categories, lead to important funding and data recovery programs when such activities take place on Federal or State lands or with government funding. Still, it has to be remembered that far more cultural resource sites are lost to these agents than are preserved, on public and private lands alike. It is a well-recognized fact of life that with the present legal, funding, and management situations, it is humanly impossible to save or investigate every prehistoric and historic site. This truism is especially evident in southwestern Colorado where thousands of cultural resource localities dot the landscape. On the positive side, though, certain forms of destructive activities, the most important for our present purposes being site vandalism, can be mitigated or alleviated through increasing the overall effectiveness of educational and protective programs. This topic will be examined later in the report.

Mention should be made of the seemingly incongruous fact that, by its very definition, the archaeological record is one which has lost important bits and pieces of critical information due to a variety of destructive processes. Schiffer (1976:27-41) provides an extended discussion concerning the processes by which the archaeological record is formed. Importantly, he notes that cultural materials suffer varying degrees of informational loss as they are transformed from a systemic or ongoing behavioral system to the archaeological context, especially those items of a perishable nature. Schiffer goes on to point out that the archaeological record may undergo changes which transform cultural materials from one state to another within the archaeological context (e.g. erosion, plowing, land leveling, etc.) and that the archaeological context may even once again return to a systemic context when the archaeologist (or vandal) retrieves the materials. Since we are only concerned with potentially destructive agents of cultural resource site and data loss, our outline corresponds to the latter two transformations of Schiffer's model: changes within the archaeological context and, more directly, the conflicts which arise as the materials come face to face with the systemic contexts of today.

Reference to Figure 2 reveals that we have divided the destructive agents to cultural resources into two major categories: natural and human-related events. We have further subdivided the human activities into "incidental" and "intentional" actions. The ensuing paragraphs briefly discuss each of these categories.

Natural Agents

Natural events which affect cultural resources are many, ranging from the effects of earthworms to volcanic and earthquake activity. Wood and Johnson (1978) have intensively reviewed a multitude of processes by which soils are mixed or otherwise altered, thereby affecting archaeological materials located within and on the deposits. Additionally, experimentation has shown the tremendous effects that may be associated with the freezing and thawing of soils (Johnson and Hansen 1974; Johnson, Muhs, and Barnhardt 1977).

In the northern Southwest, a number of natural agents act to destroy cultural resources. Predominant among these events are the consequences of erosion from wind and water, especially the actions of water erosion in the semiarid to arid climate (Fig. 3). Here, we may make special note of the harmful relationship between gullying and the results of human activities (e.g. grazing) which serve to heighten the effects of natural erosion when not checked. Another deleterious result of water action in the Four Corners area is the decimation of stone masonry walls which characterize many of the region's open and alcove sites alike. Secondarily, the flora (e.g. root systems, Fig. 4) and burrowing animals have in the past destroyed cultural information in the archaeological record, and continue to do so. It is possible to add to the list of natural agents, but those noted above can be considered to be the most destructive.

Human Agents

Man-related actions which have harmful effects on cultural resources are multitudinous and continue to increase in magnitude as lands are developed and exploited. By and large, present-day legislative

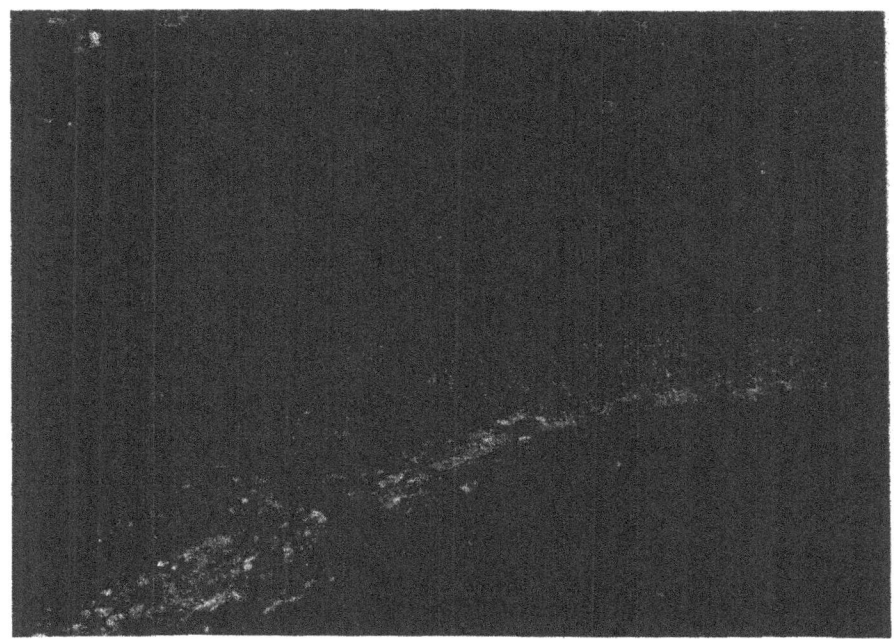

Figure 3. This photo illustrates the potential effects of natural stream erosion on 5MT4355, a large habitation site in southwestern Colorado.

Figure 4. Growth of pinyon and juniper and smaller plants can have a detrimental effect on the subsurface configuration of a site.

actions at both the Federal and State levels have been enacted to lessen or mitigate these effects on public land; however, the problems associated with certain types of activities have in no way been totally eliminated. As they pertain to cultural resources, human acts can be divided into two categories: incidental and intentional. These categories are discussed below with special attention being given to the latter. The development of a legislative base designed to curtail the destruction of cultural resources by these activities is discussed in the next chapter.

Incidental Actions

These activities may be defined as those destructive actions which are incidental to or associated with many forms of land development and exploitation. In other words, the destruction of cultural resource sites and data is not the primary motive behind such actions. These activities may be generally categorized as follows: 1) land development; 2) agriculture; 3) grazing; 4) land reclamation and flood control; 5) recreation; 6) roads, public utilities and pipelines; 7) mining and quarrying; and 8) industrial. In several instances, the precise effects of these forms of land alteration are not quantifiable for the various types of cultural resource sites which may come into conflict with such actions. It is not difficult to imagine, however, that each creates special and ultimately harmful problems for the archaeological record if allowed to continue unchecked. Seemingly, the major effects result in partial or total destruction, or at best displacement of the resources.

At the present, the literature discussing the effects of such activities is meager. Green (1974) and DeBloois, Green, and Wylie (1975), through experiments with pinyon-juniper chaining and its impact on cultural resources, found that serious effects from dragging and uprooting of trees are evident at archaeological sites. Both subsurface and surface damage to sites occurs in terms of artifact displacement, loss, breakage, and churning (Fig. 5). Much chaining in the Southwest has taken place to enhance grazing on public lands, which by

Figure 5. The consequences of pinyon-juniper woodland chaining on the surface of an archaeological site (BLM photo files).

Figure 6. Archaeological sites versus agriculture in southwestern Colorado. Site locations are indicated by unplowed areas in the field.

itself produces additional damage to cultural resources through trampling, breakage, and displacement of artifacts (Roney 1977).

The clearing and subsequent manipulation of agricultural lands has a similar if not greater effect on cultural resources (Figs. 6 through 9). While plowing is seen as basically a destructive action, in some areas it may even be an aid to the investigator who may use plowed surface scatter as an indicator for subsurface distributions (e.g. Binford et al. 1970; Roper 1976). Such is not generally the case in southwestern Colorado, however, where agricultural activities are destructive to cultural resources. As a minor but positive note, it can be observed that the only prehistoric copper bell to be recovered from southwestern Colorado was found and reported by a farmer clearing a field northwest of Cortez (Hayes and Chappell 1962), but such benefits are few and far between.

At least one article has been written which reviews the effects of a wide range of human activities on archaeological resources. In it, Vivian (1973) notes that the problem of incidental damage to cultural resources has been and continues to be great in Arizona as land-use practices increase utilization of the land.

One form of incidental effects to cultural resources on which a considerable amount of literature has accrued are detrimental actions associated with reservoir inundation (cf. Garrison 1975, 1977; Lenihan et al. 1977). Important data have been collected regarding the effects of inundation on different types of archaeological sites and the various cultural and environmental materials contained therein. In a similar vein, Schroedl (1976) has briefly documented impacts of recreation activities at Lake Powell in southeastern Utah where archaeological sites have actually become more accessible via boat traffic in the canyons. In one case, he even documented the reconstruction by visitors of a fallen wall at one alcove site in the area.

Recently, Deborah Marcus and John Noxon (personal communication to P. R. Nickens, 1980) have discussed the categories of incidental destruction (which they term "ignorant vandalism") which affect prehistoric rock art sites. They note that these types of cultural

Figure 7. Remains of a plowed site in a private field (BLM photo files)

Figure 8. This photo illustrates the process of clearing land for
agriculture using heavy equipment. The area in the
background has had the vegetation bulldozed.

Figure 9.   The consequences of land clearing practices.   In the
course of blading the access road to the acreage shown
in Figure 8, the bulldozer operator deliberately left
the road and cut through a masonry rubble mound of
prehistoric age.

resources may be adversely impacted by industrial or vehicular
pollutants and by activities related to recreational visitation, such as
touching of rock art panels.

In short summary of the problem of incidental impacts to cultural
resources associated with land alteration and use activities, it may be
said that mechanisms (e.g. legislative acts) are available to ensure that
these destructive actions do not needlessly destroy cultural resources.
Figure 10 illustrates a poignant example of this interplay at its best.
Sadly, however, not all cultural resources receive such protection,
most noticeably sites located on private land holdings. Further, as
discussed in the next section, there are those who are driven by
other motives to destructive acts, irregardless of the existence of
protective laws.

Intentional Actions

We turn now to the most important category of destructive effects
to cultural resources, at least for purposes of our discussion. Those
activities described below are especially critical for effective cultural resource management in that they are inherently harmful to the
resource and, in almost all cases, are guided by motives which are difficult to control or prevent. Intentional forms of site and data loss can
be subdivided into three categories: archaeological, predatory or
personal gain, and malicious acts. Each of these topics is briefly discussed below; additional coverage of the first two categories, and particularly the predatory category, will be included in the following
chapter when we review the historical patterns of vandalism in the
northern Southwest.

1. Archaeological Vandalism. At first glance it may appear that to
designate the activities of the professional archaeologist, whose goal
it is to retrieve data from the archaeological context and make sense
of it, as vandalistic is somewhat contradictory. Realistically, however,
it must be said that each and every archaeological endeavor leads to the
loss of varying amounts of data. This is, of course, a situation which
will never be completely mitigated since far too many factors are involved (e.g. professional competence, data retrieval techniques, time

Figure 10. This photo shows the interplay between effective cultural resource management and resource exploitation. In this instance, prehistoric sites threatened with destruction by development of a uranium processing plant in southeastern Utah are being mitigated to prevent loss of cultural resource data.

and funding constraints, to name but a few of the more important ones). Further, we must recognize that a tremendous amount of archaeological data was lost during the early phases of discovery and investigation when zeal often overshadowed scientific discretion. It is, however, difficult to castigate many of those early efforts from our present-day vantage point. Undoubtedly, our successors will at some point decry the "primitive" data recovery techniques used by archaeologists in the 1970s and 1980s and complain of the informational loss which took place.

More to the point at hand, certain archaeological practices, which unfortunately continue to exist, do result in intentional and harmful effects to the resource base. These actions range from survey techniques in which, for example, artifacts are collected without corresponding mapping of artifact loci to much more serious problems involving the use of limited research designs to guide excavation of archaeological sites. Even more serious is the act of conducting investigative work and not pursuing the necessary analysis and reporting of results steps, a practice which continues to be a bane to the profession. It is probably fair to state that in the past and even today archaeological fieldwork was/is undertaken without any intention on the part of the investigator to adequately analyze the resultant data and make it available to interested peers. Hopefully, the time has expired when well-meaning but overworked investigators are allowed to conduct more and more fieldwork beyond their capacity, professional or financial, to effectively complete the research process. As has been noted by others this practice is little more than an archaeological form of vandalism.

It can be observed, however, that such situations are waning, at least on public lands. Many factors contribute to the lessening of destructive practices by archaeologists including more effective cultural resource legislation and processing of antiquities permits, placement of archaeologists at the various levels of planning and management, and peer pressure directed toward those who continue to practice piece-meal archaeology.

2. <u>Predatory Vandalism</u>. This form of intentional activity is the most widespread and has the most serious consequences for cultural resources. It is characterized by a motive dictated by personal gain, and may be subdivided into noncommerical and commercial activities. In the first case, the effort may involve actions such as adding items to one's collection of relics, satisfying a curiosity about antiquities, or perhaps egocentric autographing of cultural resources. Commercial ventures are guided by a motive of retrieving archaeological artifacts for resale and profit.

In either case the effect to cultural resources is much the same, consisting of a long series of forms of vandalism. Williams (1977) has compiled an exhaustive listing of vandalistic practices known to occur, including the following:

<u>Form of Vandalism</u>

Excavation (digging, pothunting)

Use of heavy (construction?) machinery

Carving, scratching, chipping, general defacement

Surface collection of artifacts (especially lithic materials)

Removing, shooting at, painting, chalking, making casts and
    tracings of rock art

Theft of artifacts from structures

Stripping weathered boards or other timbers

Removing part or all of a structure or causing structural damage

Dismantling, general destruction of structure (but apparently
    no removal)

Arson

Climbing or walking on resources

Building new roads over, using modern vehicles upon historic
    roads, off-road recreational vehicle (ORRV) use

Re-arrangement of, re-locating resources

Breaking artifacts, objects, windows

Breaking and entering

Knocking structures over

Use as firewood

Throwing rocks into excavated ruin

Handling, touching

24

In order to portray the obviously detrimental effects of predatory vandalism on cultural resources in southwestern Colorado, a series of illustrations (Figs. 11 through 19) is presented at the end of this chapter. As might be expected, a majority of the literature dealing with vandalism to cultural resources deals with predatory vandalism, which of course is a worldwide problem with a long history of occurrence. Much of this literature specific to the present project will be discussed in the next chapter; however, for the interested reader, the following sources may be consulted for more in-depth information.

1. General vandalism in North America and international traffic in New World antiquities: Adams (1971); Anonymous (1977); Beals (1971); Clewlow et al. (1971); Davis (1972); Chokhani (1979); Grayson (1976); Lee (1970); Robertson (1972); Sheets (1973); and Williams (1977).

2. Vandalism in southwestern Colorado and the remainder of the Southwest: Francis (1978); Gaede and Gaede (1977); Green and LeBlanc (1979); Harden (1979); Lightfoot (1978); Lightfoot and Francis (1978); Graybill (1974); Nickens (1977); Noxon and Marcus (1980); Reyman (1979); Rippeteau (1979); Scott (1977); and Vivian (1973).

Additionally, it should be observed that the problems and consequences associated with various forms of predatory vandalism have recently been the subject of several newspaper and news magazine articles, which are generally supportive of the harmful effects of such practices. However, two examples to the contrary may be cited (Brown 1977; Hothem 1978), both of which brought about considerable protest from the professional community.

3. Malicious Vandalism. A final type of intentional vandalism, one which is difficult to precisely define, includes acts which may be classified as those brought about by revenge or frustration with governmental policies, or those which result from no discernible motive at all (Chokhani 1979:10). Fortunately, wanton or aggressive vandalism, often highly destructive in nature, occurs less frequently in comparison to other forms of activities. A recent example of senseless vandalism occurred at Arches National Park near Moab, Utah, where a highly significant rock art panel was virtually obliterated by brushing a chemical

solvent across the panel face (Noxon and Marcus 1980). The investigators commented that "this form of vandalism is most unusual in nature, being so outrageously deliberate and malicious" (Marcus and Noxon 1980, personal communication to P. R. Nickens, 1980).

Summary

The aim of the foregoing discussion has been to review the forces of destruction which act to extirpate facets of our nation's cultural heritage, and to identify those activities which are vandalistic within this context. The actions of nature upon cultural resource sites and the ever-expanding demands by populations on lands are agents of destruction which will continue to adversely affect cultural resources. It is simply not possible to halt all the detrimental actions brought about by environmental processes. These can, however, be mitigated on a case by case basis, given appropriate need and funding. It should also be noted that natural agents of destruction tend to occur more slowly than human-caused actions and therefore may be considered to have a lower overall priority in cultural resource management than those detrimental effects tied to human activities. While some problems still exist, incidental impacts to cultural resources as byproducts of land alteration and exploitation of natural resources are by and large mitigated by legislative enactments, at least on Federal and State lands. Severe problems continue to be associated with such impacts on private lands, however, with the net result that valuable vestiges of our culture history are being destroyed at an alarming rate. This fact makes it even more imperative that cultural resources on public lands be preserved and/or adequately studied.

Thus, it is the forms of intentional destruction of cultural resource sites and data on government lands which become of paramount importance. Not only do these activites result in irreversible loss of significant cultural resources, they are illegal activities in the view of past and current Federal and State legislation. Consequently, in theory anyway, such actions should be subject to preventative measures designed to ensure the integrity of the archaeological record. As we shall see, however, the determent of such activities is not an easy task.

Figure 11. Two forms of intentional vandalism to archaeological resources in southwestern Colorado. Upper - defacement of a rock art panel. Lower - scratching of graffiti in the preserved plaster covering a kiva wall in a McElmo Canyon cliff dwelling.

Figure 12. Two forms of human activity at the large Pedro Point Ruin on BLM land. Top - a recent fireplace can be seen on the slickrock in front of the ruin, built from building rubble. Bottom - prehistoric masonry blocks recently stacked to simulate a wall.

Figure 13. Vandalistic disturbance of surface artifacts in which
pottery sherds have been collected and left in a pile.

Figure 14. Pothunting of a habitation room at the large Mud Springs site, southwest of the town of Cortez (on private land).

Figure 15. This photo shows one of the clearest examples of systematic site destruction in southwestern Colorado. The site has been mined by use of a bulldozer cutting circular swaths around an immense prehistoric house, part of the Mud Spring Ruins group. Exposed walls can be seen in the cuts (on private land).

30

Figure 16. Two examples of vandalism to prehistoric ruins on public lands. Upper - pothole in a site's midden. Lower - human remains exposed by a pothunter's shovel and left to decay.

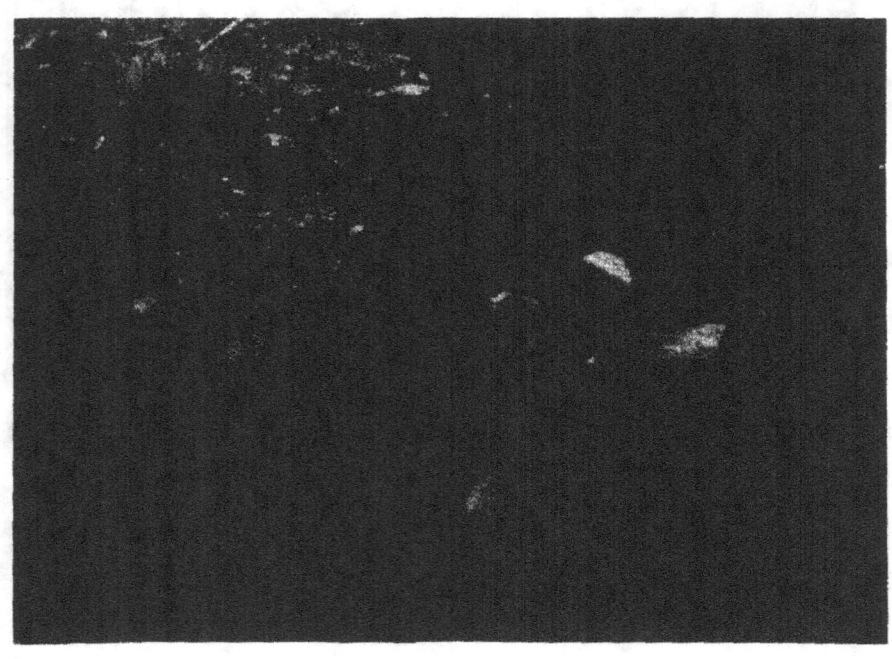

Figure 17. Other forms of vandalistic actions at ruins on public lands. Top - potted and exposed upright slab storage cist. Bottom - person is kneeling in a bulldozer cut through a midden.

Figure 18.   BLM San Juan Resource Area archaeologist Gary Matlock
surveys damage done to a site by random potholes.

Figure 19. Montrose District BLM archaeologist Douglas Scott
inspecting a motorbike trail leading to a small
cliff dwelling in McElmo Canyon.

Figure 20. Remains of a recently unearthed human skeleton are examined by Steve Fuller, a BLM archaeologist stationed in southwestern Colorado.

III

HISTORICAL OVERVIEW OF CULTURAL RESOURCE
DESTRUCTION IN SOUTHWESTERN COLORADO

General

This chapter seeks to examine historical patterns of deliberate or intentional despoilation of archaeological sites in southwestern Colorado and, to a lesser extent, similar contemporaneous events occurring in neighboring regions. By necessity the account must depend on the written record, which includes the views of early archaeologists on the problem, biographies of explorers and collectors, diaries, and other documentation. Without a doubt, much of the early activity of this type went unrecorded and the full extent of the problem cannot be properly understood. This is especially true for the period following passage of the Antiquities Act of 1906 which ostensibly provided protection for archaeological sites on public lands controlled by the Federal government. There is, simply put, very little in the way of documentation concerning vandalistic activities taking place over the past 75 years. Nevertheless, it will be painfully evident that a tremendous amount of such activity took place within the short time covered by the last two decades of the nineteenth century when interest in collectable Anasazi antiquities was rampant.

It is anticipated that several salient aspects pertaining to the general problem of destruction of archaeological sites and data will be evident. One of these points will involve the intensity and scale of early exploration and collecting ventures which, when fully realized, is particularly alarming. The resultant collections lie today, virtually undocumented, in many of the country's museums and it is only fair to place partial blame on some of these institutions which at the time were more concerned with filling shelves and display cases than with proper description of the collection's origins. Another very important result to be derived from the historical overview is a perspective that the ethic of accumulating prehistoric antiquities, both for personal collections and for profit, is a deeply-rooted and enduring cultural tradition in southwestern Colorado, one as old as the initial settlement of the area itself. This facet of the overall problem, perhaps more than any other, is critical to understanding the viewpoint of local residents toward cultural resources.

For the sake of discussion, historical patterns of site destruction may be subdivided into three convenient temporal periods: 1) exploration up to 1885; 2) 1886 to about 1900; and 3) ca. 1901 until the present. Although there is overlap in the motives for such activities during these periods, there are enough differences in the scope of work to validate the delineations. A more detailed accounting of archaeological investigations during the entire time frame may be found in the recent cultural resources overview for southwestern Colorado (Nickens 1980), and a description of the concomitant historical developments for the area has been written by O'Rourke (1980). Interested readers are encouraged to consult these sources for additional information.

Archaeological Site Destruction: Exploration to 1885

It is probably realistic to state that prehistoric resources in southwestern Colorado have been faced with cumulative incidental and intentional impacts from human activities dating from the first Spanish expeditions during the last half of the 1700s. Journals from both the Rivera expeditions (1761-1765) and the Dominguez-Escalante trek in 1776 contain notations on the presence of numerous ancient pueblos observed along the trail. Although no record of digging in the ruins was noted by the chroniclers, we may expect that some disturbance to the antiquities may have occurred.

If we were to be even more precise about the matter of who were the first to disturb prehistoric Anasazi sites in southwestern Colorado, however, we would have to point to the Southern Ute groups who occupied the area at the time of Spanish contact and into historic times. Apparently a prevalent practice of the Utes was the gathering of a wide variety of stone implements, and even pottery on occasion, from the surfaces of prehistoric sites for reuse (Nickens 1980:114).

38

Regardless of who the initial disturbers of archaeological sites
were, it can be stated that impacts to the sites were minimal prior to
the mid 1880s, even by those who dug in the ruins for antiquities.
The first documentation of actual excavation in the ruins of southwestern
Colorado comes from the reports of investigators with the Hayden surveys of
the area between the years of 1874-1876. W. H. Holmes, the geologist on
the 1875 and 1876 expeditions, refers in his report to digging activities
in the cliff dwellings along the Mancos River, south of the present-day
Mesa Verde National Park (Holmes 1878). In a later publication dealing
with the pottery collected from the ruins, Holmes (1886:284-285) recounts
the excitement of discovery which gripped these earliest diggers. He
writes:

> ...I made it a point to camp for the night directly below
> these houses (cliff dwellings)...The two finest houses were
> set in shallow, wind-worn caves, several hundred feet above
> the valley.
>
> I had ascended alone and was busily engaged in studying
> the upper house and tracing the plans of its fallen walls,
> when I heard a voice echoing among the cliffs. Descending
> hastily to the lower house I found that one of my men had
> followed me and was excitedly scratching with a stick among
> the debris of fallen walls. He had just discovered the rim
> of a buried pot, and was fairly breathless from the antici-
> pation of "piles of moons." By the aid of my geologic
> hammer we soon had the upper part of the neck uncovered,
> but hesitated a moment with bated breath before venturing
> to raise the rough stone lid. But there was no treasure--
> only a heap of dust. I was content, however, and when by
> a little further search we came upon a second vessel, a
> mate to the first, the momentary shades of disappointment
> vanished.

The accounts of Holmes and his contemporary and fellow surveyor
on the Hayden expeditions, William H. Jackson, led to extended mention
of southwestern Colorado's prehistoric ruins in two widely read and
used travel books. One of these was written by Ernest Ingersoll (1885),
who had accompanied Jackson during the 1874 survey. The second was
Crofutt's "Grip-sack Guide of Colorado" (1885) which relies entirely
on Holmes' earlier discussion of the ancient ruins in Colorado to
encourage travelers to be sure and include these monuments of past

civilizations in their itinerary. What effects such accounts had on increasing visitation to the ruins is not known. It is likely, however, that the ruins received little impact from this early calling of attention to their presence and splendor.

As an aside, it should be noted that although the cultural resources in southwestern Colorado remained relatively untouched prior to 1885, other areas of the Southwest were being subjected to destructive activities. In his 1886 treatise on Southwestern pottery, for example, Holmes (1886) discusses a large collection of prehistoric ceramic vessels taken from several locations in southwestern Utah in 1876 and placed in the National Museum.

Another early example of cultural resource destruction took place at Pecos Pueblo, located east of Santa Fe, New Mexico, a historically-abandoned Indian village and Spanish church. There, as Kessell (1979) relates, the pueblo and church fell prey to pothunters, scavengers, and transients as beams, many elaborately carved and painted, were torn from the buildings for use as firewood and in building houses, stables, and corrals. An early investigator of the day, Adolf Bandelier, described the ravaging of the site as follows:

> In general, the vandalism committed in this venerable relic of antiquity defies all description. It is only equalled by the foolishness of such as, having no other means to secure immortality, have cut out the ornaments from the sculptured beams in order to obtain a surface suitable to carve their euphonious names. All the beams of the old structure are quaintly, but still not tastelessly, carved; there was...much scroll-work terminating them. Most of this was taken away, chipped into uncouth boxes, and sold, to be scattered everywhere. Not content with this, treasure-hunters, inconsiderate amateurs, have recklessly and ruthlessly disturbed the abodes of the dead (Bandelier 1881:42).

In spite of the tragedy as described by Bandelier, some good resulted from the account as the Eastern establishment became aroused and concerned at the destruction. Lee (1970) observes that Bandelier's article greatly aided the newly born fight to pass legislation to protect antiquities on federal lands. Sadly, however, it would be another 25 years before such action would be completed. In the meantime, the years 1886-1900 were to be critical ones for archaeological sites in the Southwest, and especially so for those in southwestern Colorado.

Archaeological Site Destruction: 1886-1900

The events surrounding the settlement of southwestern Colorado and the subsequent growth of interest in the antiquities, particularly those situated in the sheltered alcoves of the area's canyons, are well known (e.g. Chapin 1892; Nordenskiold 1893; McNitt 1957; Fletcher 1977) and need not be retold here. The story centers around the activities of the Wetherill family of Mancos, which in addition to running cattle in the huge Mancos Canyon and its tributaries, spent considerable time exploring the canyon walls to discover cliff dwellings. It must be stated, however, that numerous other explorers and collecting parties were also active in the area during this time, especially after word of the Wetherills' discoveries was made known.

All in all, the period from 1886 to 1900 was an extremely catastrophic time for cultural resources in the entire Four Corners area. From the first discoveries of the larger and richer sites--in terms of preserved artifacts--came the ultimate realization that profits could be made by amassing collections for sale to wealthy philanthropists and museums throughout the country. Typically, each of these many collections consisted of hundreds or even thousands of prehistoric relics including human remains, pottery, baskets, stone, wooden, and bone implements, and textiles. States even got into the act as both Colorado and Utah commissioned collectors to hurriedly amass suitable collections of cliff-dweller artifacts for the 1893 World's Fair in Chicago. The Wetherills had two of their Mesa Verde collections exhibited at the Fair, one collected for the State and another earlier one which had been privately purchased.

Unfortunately, other activities detrimental to archaeological sites were occurring simultaneously with the amassing of large collections. Of even more concern is the fact that little is known of the extent and results of these ancillary situations. One of these was an intensive desire on the part of citizens to see the ruins and their hidden riches. In all fairness, many of those who came probably did so only to view the spectacular ruins, but undoubtedly many left the area with momentos of their visits to the cliff dwellings.

In addition to their own exploring and collecting actions, the Wetherills engaged in guiding tourists to the Mesa Verde ruins, running newspaper advertisements catering to the tourist trade. Fletcher (1977) observes that between 1889 and 1901 nearly one thousand persons signed the visitor register at the Wetherill ranch. Prices charged by the Wetherills ranged from $5.00 for a one-day trip to ruins in Mancos Canyon, to $20.00 for a three-day excursion to the major sites of Mesa Verde, and $30.00 to $40.00 for a longer foray to the Hovenweep area. Tourists came from throughout the United States and many European countries. It can only be surmised how many others who did not register with the Wetherills visited the area's ruins during this time. It may be expected that the number was considerable, not to mention the local residents who made visits as well.

It was also during this time that the local tradition of pot-hunting began among residents of the area. In some cases, extra needed cash could be had for artifacts and, in other instances, a desire for personal collections provided the motive. Much of this sort of activity was undoubtedly a result of land clearing and tilling actions, but much of it was viewed simply as a pastime or sport. As might be expected, there is little in the way of documentation of such activities. T. Mitchell Prudden, a medical doctor who devoted much attention to scientific inquiry of the prehistoric sites in the area, made the following striking comments which portray the situation.

> For any one who chooses now to gather them, the ancient pottery and other utensils...have considerable value for purposes of sale...It is the practice of the settlers, on Sundays or other holidays, to organize picnics to the ruins. And the rustic swain is wont to signalize his regard for his Dulcinea by digging for her out of the desolate graves what articles the chances of the hour may bring. She cozily seated amid piles of broken pottery, darting lizards, and dead men's bones, smiles complacently... (Prudden 1896:552).

> (In the Hovenweep area)...few mounds have escaped the
> hands of the destroyer. Cattlemen, ranchmen, rural pic-
> nickers, and professional collectors have turned the
> ground well over and have taken much pottery, breaking
> more, and strewing the ground with many crumbling bones
> (Prudden 1903:263).

One consequence of these activities was that open surface sites which, when compared to the cliff dwellings, presented relatively difficult digging began to be exploited. Part of the reason for a shifting interest in open rubble mounds may be attributed to the extant economic situation. First, the more lucrative cliff dwellings were rapidly exploited. McNitt (1975:32) observes that by Richard Wetherill's own count he, alone or with his brothers, had explored some 182 cliff dwellings in the Mesa Verde area by 1890. Thus, the return at these sites was considerably reduced in a hurry. During the early 1890s, there was also an economic slump leading up to the Silver Panic of 1893, when the United States adopted the gold standard. Aware of the substantial returns the Wetherills and others were reaping for their collections of antiquities, many settlers turned to artifact collecting, which they considered as yet another natural resource to be exploited (Lister and Lister 1968:4). Similarly, a short-lived gold rush in the Glen Canyon of southeastern Utah (see Crampton 1964) brought many people to the area who, after the gold played out, also turned to relic hunting in the rich ruins found in the canyon tributaries of the San Juan and Colorado Rivers. Realizing the richness of sites such as those in Grand Gulch, the Wetherills also turned their attentions to this area in the mid-1890s.

According to the available accounts, by 1895 the heavy commercial ventures in antiquities had died a welcome death in southwestern Colorado and southeastern Utah. In large measure, this event was associated with the diminishing returns from the extensively excavated cave sites. Also, however, important to this demise was an awakening on the part of many to the scientific value of conserving the rapidly disappearing resources, or at least to the fact that scientific investigation of archaeological sites was in the best interest of the resource base and the nation.

Richard Wetherill foresaw this turn of events when he commented in a letter to one of his sponsors, B. Talbot Hyde, in 1897 that "...all work in Arizona ruins is prohibited. New Mexico is waking up to that point also" (letter on file at the American Museum of Natural History, New York).

To close our discussion of the widespread and uncontrolled destruction of archaeological sites in the northern Southwest during this period, we can note the following written comments of early scientists, who were, quite appropriately, alarmed at the unprofessional goings on of the period. To an extent, these comments provide an adequate summary of the amount of cultural resource site and data loss which occurred during the last two decades of the nineteenth century.

> ...as a rule the Southwestern ruins are now suffering more from the white man than from the Indian. If this destruction of the cliff houses of New Mexico, Colorado, and Arizona goes on at the same rate in the next fifty years as it has in the past, these unique dwellings will be practically destroyed and unless laws are enacted, either by states or by the general government, for their protection, at the close of the twentieth century (19th ?) many of the most interesting monuments of the prehistoric people of our Southwest will be little more than mounds of debris at the bases of cliffs. A commercial spirit is leading to careless excavations for objects to sell, and walls are ruthlessly overthrown, buildings torn down in hopes of a few dollars gain. The proper designation of the way our antiquities are treated is vandalism. Students who follow us, when these cliff houses have all disappeared and their instructive objects scattered by the greed of traders, will wonder at our indifference and designate our negligence by its proper name. It would be wise legislation to prevent this vandalism as much as possible and good science to put all excavation of ruins in trained hands (Fewkes 1896:269-270).

> The great hindrance to successful archaeological work in this region lies in the fact that there is scarcely an ancient dwelling site or cemetery that has not been vandalized by "pottery diggers" for gain (Hough 1901:590).

> The pueblo-like cliff dwellings being situated under heavy, overhanging ledges are well protected from the elements and unmolested would endure for centuries. But their destruction seems to have been made the peculiar pasttime of a certain class of human beings. The early explorers of the Mancos Canyon would now find, in many cases, unrecognizable heaps of

stone where thirty years ago were well preserved structures. The excavation of cliff dwellings without due regard to the preservation of walls should be made a grave misdemeanor (Hewett 1904).

Most of the ruins of the Southwest are given over today to unbridled vandalism. A pot or a skull is worth a few dimes to a trader and a few dollars to a tourist, and so has been evolved the holiday and professional pot-hunter. Everywhere the ruins are ravaged. More is destroyed in the search than is saved. No records are kept (Prudden 1907:172).

Probably no cliff dwelling in the Southwest has been more thoroughly dug over in search of pottery and other objects for commercial purposes than Cliff Palace. Parties of "curio seekers" camped in the ruin for several winters, and it is reported that many hundred specimens therefrom have been carried down the mesa and sold to private individuals. Some of these objects are now in museums but many are forever lost to science. In order to secure this valuable archaeological material, walls were broken down with powder, often simply to let light into the darker rooms; floors were invariably opened and buried kivas mutilated. To facilitate this work and get rid of the dust, great openings were broken through the fine walls which form the front of the ruin. Beams were used for firewood to so great an extent that not a single roof now remains. This work of destruction, added to that resulting from erosion due to rain, left Cliff Palace in a sad condition (Annual Report of the Secretary of the Interior for 1909:486 [quoted in Ise 1961:145]).

Cultural Resource Destruction and Protection: 1901 to the Present

As a result of the events of the latter part of the nineteenth century, principally the large-scale destruction of archaeological sites on public lands in the Southwest, major legislative steps were taken soon after the turn of the century to halt such activities. In 1906, a much-debated Antiquities Act was signed by President Theodore Roosevelt. For the interested, Lee (1970) has provided a detailed account of prior events and passage of this act. The most important features of this act were as follows: 1) all antiquities on lands owned or controlled by the Federal government were given protection; 2) the President was given authority to declare "national monuments," providing additional protection to important antiquities; 3) the

Secretaries of Interior, War, and Agriculture were given authority to grant excavation permits, thereby initiating control over investigators as well as investigations of archaeological sites on these lands; and 4) penalties were provided for violations of the Act's provisions. While this legislation was a milestone at the time of passage, as we shall see later it did not provide the long term protection hoped for by its authors and supporters.

In southwest Colorado, Mesa Verde National Park was created in the same year to preserve what was left of the spectacular cliff dwellings. It was not designated as an archaeological preserve under terms of the Antiquities Act since legislation to create the Park had been introduced earlier. Subsequently, two other smaller areas in southwestern Colorado, Yucca House and Hovenweep, were designated as Monuments in 1919 and 1923, respectively.

It is difficult to assess the impact the Antiquities Act had on illegal digging in the years after its passage. Judging from the level of appropriations, staffing, and the length of time it took to properly develop the park and monuments in southwestern Colorado, it is difficult to imagine that even minimal enforcement of the Antiquities Act would have been possible. The senior author of this report has inspected a prehistoric human skeleton and accompanying grave goods in a local collection which were purportedly excavated from an unknown locale in Mesa Verde National Park in 1919, well after establishment of the Park.

Meanwhile, it may be expected that pothunting and destruction of sites continued on private and public lands in southwestern Colorado. During the 1930s, the problem came to the forefront once more, perhaps again in part a consequence of national economic decline. The Listers (Lister and Lister 1968:161-162) have summarized this episode in the following manner.

> The decade of the 30's witnessed one of the most virulent epidemics of pothunting ever to sweep any section of the San Juan. The center of the outbreak was concentrated in the upper Animas valley of southern Colorado. Here signs of the ancient ones were not spectacular. Yet from the first thrust of white penetration into the region in the 1870's occasional finds of Indian relics had been made.

They were so rare and generally without individuality that they excited little interest in a public impressed only by the biggest or the oldest, one of which lay unknown at the town's limits.

With a growing awareness of the tremendously rich archaeological finds coming to light elsewhere in the San Juan basin, local weekend collectors formed a society where enthusiasm and knowledge could be pooled. They were met with unexpected success as reports of more and more ruins were made, and collections of artifacts grew to sizeable proportions...

Archaeologists, lacking the strengthening rod of law, sought to stem the tide of potting by preaching. Too often their manner was either condescending or threatening. The reaction in the collector ranks was defiance and hostility, resulting in fortified determination to continue the Sunday hobby regardless of antipathy in certain quarters. Many pursued the avocation because of the love of the quest. Others were genuinely interested in the study of the Indians. A few, mistakingly believing the oldness meant remunerative value, saw what was hoped to be a chance to pick up some extra cash. These were the ones inadvertently encouraged in their digging for relics by the professionals themselves who bought collections rather than see them dispersed into a dozen channels.

To our knowledge, no written documentation exists which discusses vandalism of archaeological sites in southwestern Colorado between ca. 1940 and the past few years, although it can be stated that such activities were ongoing. Several large privately-owned collections have been amassed over the past generation. Two examples of such collections which have been donated to public repositories may be cited as evidence. One, the Hoofnagle Collection, was donated to the University of Colorado in the early 1960s by the widow of the collector, who had been an employee of the U.S. Forest Service in the Durango area (Afton 1971). Among other items, it included more than 60 ceramic vessels taken from at least 32 excavated burials from the Yellowjacket site, located 15 miles west of Cortez. Another collection, known as the Mellinger Collection, was donated to the Colorado Historical Society in 1950 (J. A. Heberling, personal communication to P. R. Nickens, 1978). This collection, from southwestern Colorado and southeastern Utah, contains numerous examples of pottery and human remains, including three mummies from Grand Gulch, Utah.

These are but two examples of the practice of amassing personal collections; many others are known to exist, both as donated collections and those still in private hands. Obviously, the motives behind certain collecting activities are not entirely economic. On the other hand, occasionally the opposite is true. Recently, a large collection of prehistoric pottery vessels numbering more than 1000 specimens, gathered by private collectors from southeastern Utah, was purchased by the State of Utah for $40,000. The local newspaper account of the transaction made no mention of the amount, however, noting only that the "citizens" turned over the collections for display at the local state museum. Additional viewpoints of recent and ongoing artifact collecting actions gained from interviews will be presented in Chapter V.

Thus, it can be accepted that although not much is known about the actual circumstances, the collecting of antiquities in southwestern Colorado, both in legal and illegal contexts, has continued unabated over the past several decades. Only in the past few years have reliable indications of the ongoing vandalism to cultural resources on public lands in the area begun to appear. These revelations have resulted from increased awareness on the part of professionals and land managers who, recognizing the problem is a serious one, have sought to strengthen the laws prohibiting vandalism to cultural resources.

These concerns stem directly from the realization that prehistoric and historic remains are deserving of the same degree of protection as other environmental resources. This movement, generally known under the rubric of "cultural resource management," involves combined efforts at all levels to ensure that, in spite of increasing use of public lands and conflicts with the conservation and preservation of archaeological sites and information, these resources are accorded adequate protection. The loss of data due to vandalism is one of the concerns of cultural resource management and in some areas, such as the BLM Sacred Mountain Planning Unit, it is a relatively important one.

The past few years have been significant to the topic of protecting cultural resources in southwestern Colorado from vandalistic activities as increased levels of awareness about the overall problem have surfaced.

In the case of the BLM, this awakening has brought the Bureau closer to fulfilling the obligations concerning the protection of antiquities as vested in them by the Secretary of the Interior. It should be noted that although we are primarily discussing illegal destruction of sites on public land at this point, the problem of protection and management of cultural resources is a multifaceted one due to the many demands currently being placed on public lands. However, the problem of vandalism is one of the most difficult situations to control due to its nature and, therefore, creates enormous management concern.

One of the most critical aids to the prevention of vandalism has been the strengthening of statutory authority to protect cultural resources on public lands and the willingness on the part of the government to prosecute violators of the laws. In the mid-1970s, when serious prosecution of antiquities violations began to take place, it was rather quickly realized that the Antiquities Act of 1906 was not the panacea once believed, as it was ruled to be unconstitutionally vague in several court cases involving cultural resource vandals. Hence, once the long overdue enforcement of the law was finally attempted, serious questions about the ability to implement penalties against vandals quickly came to the forefront. Further, as Anderson (1978:3) has pointed out, the moderate penalties of a $500.00 fine and a sentence of not more than 90 days, or both, imposed under the 1906 Act meant little to the vandal who could get several thousand dollars for a single pottery vessel from the right buyer. Consequently, the risk of a small fine and/or a brief sentence could be considered an "overhead" expense to looters. If the protection of the nation's cultural heritage was to become a meaningful effort, a modernized antiquities act was sorely needed (Collins and Green 1978).

After considerable debate, the Archaeological Resources Protection Act of 1979 (P.L. 96-95-Oct 31, 1979) was passed to fill this requirement. Violations of the 1979 act carry penalties of a fine of up to $10,000 and imprisonment of up to one year, or both. However, if the commercial or archaeological value of the archaeological resources involved and the cost of restoration and repair of such resources exceeds the sum of $5000.00, the guilty party(ies) may be liable for a fine of not more than $20,000 or imprisonment of two years, or both. In the case of repeated offenses, the fine may be increased to not more than $100,000, or a sentence of up to five years, or both. The penalties provided under this act take on meaning when it is remembered that the value of a single vessel illegally excavated from an archaeological site in some areas may exceed the $5000.00 limit, not to mention the cost of restoration and repair of the site itself. Hopefully, successful convictions under the new act will quickly become a strong deterrent to such activities.

In addition to strengthening the law covering looting of archaeological sites, another positive situation in the past few years has been increased publicity about the seriousness of the problem and the consequences of such activities to both the vandal and the resource base. There has been a recent proliferation of newspaper and magazine articles, educational films, and pamphlets, all designed to acquaint the general public with the impacts and deleterious effects of these activities. We have also witnessed long overdue written disapproval from the professional archaeological community. Fittingly, a majority of the professional articles on the problems of vandalism are being written by archaeologists involved with providing direct input to management decisions concerning cultural resources.

The dissemination of information on the motives, methods, and consequences is extremely important to arriving at solutions to the problems associated with vandalistic activities. Only in this manner do we begin to more fully realize the seriousness of the situation, and if the problem is to be alleviated, the symptoms creating it have to be recognized. Thus, for southwestern Colorado a brief article by Douglas Scott, a BLM archaeologist, served to call attention to vandalism of archaeological sites. Scott (1977) observed that two key factors seemed to contribute greatly to vandalism: visibility of the resource and accessibility via existing road networks. As to solutions, he suggested patrolling of existing roads, fencing of important sites, control over new road construction and closure of unnecessary roads, public education programs, and prosecution of apprehended vandals.

In a more recent report, Fred Harden (1979), a seasonal ranger in the BLM San Juan Resource Area, notes that a wide variety of tools and equipment is being utilized to find and excavate antiquities on public lands. Included in this array are CB radios as warning systems against apprehension, ski poles as probes, screens to sift out artifacts from excavations, and off-road vehicles to gain access to sites. On occasion, other techniques which might be used involve working at night to avoid detection, use of aircraft to help identify site locations, and employing heavy equipment such as bulldozers. Harden further notes that factors causing vandalism include the following: 1) the availability of local markets for artifacts; 2) the fact that benefits outweigh the risks (i.e. under the Antiquities Act of 1906); and 3) availability of easy access. Like Scott, Harden advocated education, controlling access, and more effective law enforcement as management recommendations, along with stressing a need for legislative action to replace the vague 1906 Act. Noting that about twenty sites were observed to have been vandalized during the summer of 1979, Harden states that vandalism in the Sacred Mountain Planning Unit is increasing, although the basis for this observation is not clear in his report.

Two other recent articles have brought about attention to vandalistic activities in southwestern Colorado. Reyman (1979) pointed out site destruction which is taking place at some national parks and monuments, including Mesa Verde. Reyman points to activities such as visitors creating "new" sites (e.g. rock art symbols), theft of display artifacts and other souvenirs, and defacement (graffiti). Alarmed by such acts occurring in designated archaeological preserves, he advocates a threefold approach to the problem: 1) education of federal government personnel about the problem; 2) increased involvement of archaeologists in educating the public about the need to preserve sites; and 3) formation of a national conference to deal with the vandalism problem. The second article (Rippeteau 1979) reviewed the enforcement of antiquities laws, both Federal and State, in Colorado, outlining past and continuing efforts of agencies and law enforcement officials to prosecute vandals of cultural resources. Both of these statements, along with those of

Scott and Harden, have greatly contributed to publicizing the problem and, importantly, have contributed various suggestions to help combat its serious effects to our cultural heritage.

Summary

To briefly recapitulate, the history of vandalism and destruction to cultural resources exhibits an unbroken tradition, lasting from the first settlement of the area to the present. Over this span, the apparent motives have been many--curiosity, commercial, hobby collecting, and outright malicious acts. We may note that the two most serious outbreaks of commercial vandalism coincided with worsening national-economic conditions. Some feel that the commercial aspect of pothunting is a prime mover behind such activities in many parts of the Southwest today. In other cases, the feeling of pride, in local history and in being a successful hunter and collector of relics, provides sufficient motivation and is an end in itself for such acts. These two forms of predatory vandalism undoubtedly comprise a majority of destructive activities.

Despite the ongoing seriousness of the overall problem, positive and significant steps have been taken in recent years to help eradicate the actions of the vandal. These measures include an increased aware-ness of the situation by land managers and archaeologists, publicity of the losses caused by such acts, and greater potential penalties for those apprehended and prosecuted for destructive deeds.

IV

DATA PRESENTATION: KNOWN SITE INFORMATION

General

To accomplish the goal of defining and evaluating factors affecting
archaeological site vandalism in the Sacred Mountain Planning Unit,
several approaches were outlined. In general terms, these lines of
inquiry may be listed as follows: 1) compilation of data from existing
site files and previous investigations; 2) a brief field check of some
previously recorded sites to provide supplementary information; and
3) informant interviews with persons who reside in the project area and
are known to be artifact collectors. The results of the known site data
compilations and field implementation efforts are discussed below, while
a summation of the informant interview phase is presented in the following chapter. Together, these bodies of data form the basis for statements
concerning factors important to a better understanding of the vandalism
problem and for subsequent recommendations to aid in the prevention of
such activities.

Several stages of work were outlined to review data contained in
the cultural resource site file and other existing information. First,
a set of variables thought to be important to the vandalism problem was
derived and the comprehensive site file at the BLM Montrose District
office was examined in light of these variables. Following tabulation
of these results for sites on BLM lands, they were compared to a similar
analysis of nearly 300 prehistoric sites recorded during the recent
class II cultural resource inventory of the Sacred Mountain Planning Unit
(Chandler, Reed, and Nickens 1980). This survey, completed during
1978-79, was a stratified proportional probability sample of some 8000
acres, or about four percent, of the Planning Unit. Although the primary
goal of that work was to provide a statistically reliable projection of
the density and types of cultural resources on public lands in the area,
site recording techniques also included collection of data relevant to
vandalism aspects. The results of the class II inventory, then, comprise
a reliable and convenient data base for comparative purposes. Finally, a

sample of previously known sites which had originally been recorded as pristine (i.e. unvandalized) was selected and revisited to assess rates and forms of ongoing vandalism and to verify the data contained in the site files. An ancillary goal of the field implementation phase was to field test a format for more precise recording of vandalism and associated variables. The collection of such data will be critical to future analyses of archaeological site vandalism.

Known Site Data

Methods

A number of variables, measurable at prehistoric sites, were selected for analysis prior to data compilation. These include the following categories: 1) age/cultural period of the site; 2) type of site; 3) distance to nearest road; 4) type of nearest access road; 5) distance to nearest town. As might be expected, placement of known site data into these categories was at times difficult as many previously recorded sites lacked certain information pertaining to one or more variables. Nonetheless, after sites with incomplete or unknown data entries were culled from the total number of known sites, adequate samples for analysis remained in both the BLM site file source and the class II inventory data base. In some cases, the absence of information was minor and the sites were included in analysis of certain variables, causing slight variation in some totals.

Comparisons were made for each variable measured between vandalized and unvandalized sites. The criterion for defining vandalism was the presence of some form of intentional human activity causing destruction of a site and/or data. For example, forms of vandalism noted included illegal excavation (potholes) and defacement of rock art sites. In many instances, site recorders did not adequately document the presence or absence of vandalism; however, if the site photo clearly indicated potholes or other disturbances the site was coded as being vandalized. Surface collecting, a prevalent form of vandalism, was all but impossible to discern from the site forms and, thus, cannot be included in the analysis.

Whenever possible, data on other variables was also collected. One of these was whether or not a site which was formally noted on a U.S.G.S.

quadrangle map as a "ruin" had been vandalized. Another was the area of the site which exhibited vandalism (e.g. midden area versus roomblocks). The results of these compilations are reviewed following presentation of data related to site age, type, and access vis à vis vandalism activities.

Results

Site Age and Type

These two variables are closely linked with few exceptions. Generally speaking, the earlier sites lack the characteristic highly visible rubble mounds denoting ruins of surface masonry structures. There is a decided trend for the later sites with masonry rubble to have been vandalized. Of the prehistoric sites recorded during the class II inventory, 41% of the sites with masonry had been damaged while only 21% of the non-masonry sites had been vandalized. Correspondingly, 48% of the late period Anasazi sites (McElmo and Mesa Verde phases) had been vandalized as compared to 27% of the middle period sites (Ackmen and Mancos phases) and only 11% of early period sites (La Plata and Piedra phases). A total of 54% of late sites with masonry architecture had been vandalized.

Of the previously recorded sites, a similar trend is indicated as shown in the following tabulation.

Cultural period	No. of sites in sample	No. vandalized	% vandalized
Basketmaker II-III	74	9	12%
Pueblo I	158	24	15%
Pueblo II	172	38	22%
Pueblo II-III	239	103	43%
Pueblo III	89	28	31%
TOTALS	732	202	28%

Of the 202 vandalized sites noted above, 4% are Basketmaker II-III, 12% are Pueblo I, 19% are Pueblo II, 51% are Pueblo II-III, and 14% are Pueblo III.

In terms of site type, such designations are highly variable on the BLM site file forms and, consequently, only the data from the class II inventory are presented in full. These are as follows:

Site type	No. unvandalized/ % of total		No. vandalized/ % of total	
Surface Pueblo	39	(55%)	27	(68%)
Pithouse	10	(14%)	1	(2.5%)
Tower	4	(6%)	3	(7%)
Granary	1	(1%)	2	(5%)
Cist	1	(1%)	1	(2.5%)
Cliff dwelling	2	(3%)	1	(2.5%)
Rockshelter	11	(16%)	4	(10%)
Field house	1	(1%)	0	0
Kiva	2	(3%)	1	(2.5%)
TOTALS	71	(100%)	40	(100%)

The following percentages of each type were noted as having been vandalized, albeit many types have too few occurrences to be regarded as accurate samples or estimates.

Site type	No.	No. vandalized	% vandalized
Surface pueblo	66	27	41%
Pithouse	11	1	9%
Tower	7	3	42%
Granary	3	2	67%
Cist	2	1	50%
Cliff dwelling	3	1	33%
Rockshelter	15	4	27%
Field house	1	0	0
Kiva	3	1	33%
TOTALS	71	40	

Incidences of vandalism at two special types of sites, cliff dwellings and rock art, were possible to tally from the BLM site files. A total of 37 cliff dwellings dating to the Pueblo II and III period have been previously recorded, of which 26 (70%) had been vandalized. A review of rock art sites of indeterminate age revealed that of 15 recorded instances, seven (47%) had been vandalized, all in the form of having graffiti scratched on their surfaces.

Thus, we see that the later, more visible Anasazi sites have been subjected to heavier vandalism in the past. This distribution is not unexpected.

Access to Sites

This general category is thought to be one of the primary factors affecting vandalism in the Sacred Mountain Planning Unit (Scott 1977).

Three variables were measured to evaluate the association between access and vandalism: 1) distance to nearest road; 2) type of nearest road; and 3) distance to nearest town. Type of road was categorized from U.S.G.S. topographic maps and BLM road update maps in the following manner:

Rank	Type of road
1	Paved, state or county
2	Gravel
3	Dirt with ditch
4	Dirt with berm
5	Track or jeep trail

The results of these measurements and analyses are broken down between the class II inventory sites (those with architecture only) and site data contained in the BLM files.

1. Class II inventory sites

The mean distance to unvandalized sites from the nearest road is 580 m, with a range of 100 m to 1.3 km. The mean distance to vandalized sites from the nearest road is 491 m, with a range of 10 m to 3.0 km. When distances are grouped into five ranges, an x^2 analysis shows the differences between vandalized and unvandalized sites to be significant at .01. Distances were grouped as follows: visible from the road (≤ 100 m), a short walk from the road (101-400 m), a moderately short walk from the road (401-800 m), a moderately long walk from the road (0.8 - 1.6 km), and a long walk from the road (over 1.6 km).

Distance to Roads

	≤ 100 m	101-400 m	401-800 m	0.8-1.6 km	over 1.6 km	
Vandalized	12 (86%)	11 (38%)	12 (33%)	4 (27%)	1 (100%)	40 (42%)
Unvandalized	2 (14%)	18 (62%)	24 (67%)	11 (73%)	0 (0)	55 (58%)
	14	29	36	15	1	95

$$x^2 = 15.22 \qquad df = 4 \qquad p < .01$$

The proximity of a site to town does not appear to increase its probability of being vandalized, as only 38% of sites within 16 km of the nearest town had been vandalized, as compared to 73% of sites over 32 km

57

from the nearest town. 38% of sites 17-32 km from town had been vandalized. However, an x^2 analysis reveals that the differences between vandalized and unvandalized sites are significant at 0.10. A higher number of vandalized sites than expected are located over 32 km from the nearest town.

Distance to Nearest Town

	Vandalized	Unvandalized	
$\leq$ 16 km	10 (38%)	16 (62%)	26
17-32 km	22 (38%)	36 (62%)	58
over 32 km	8 (73%)	3 (27%)	11
	40	55	95

$$x^2 = 4.16 \qquad df = 2 \qquad p < .10$$

More sites are located near dirt and two-track roads (ranks 4 and 5) than near improved roads; none of the sites recorded on the Sacred Mountain Project was located near a road with a rank higher than 3. There is a significant difference between vandalized and unvandalized sites with respect to rank of nearest road, with the highest percentage of vandalized sites located near rank 4 roads. The highest percentage of unvandalized sites are located near two-track jeep trails (rank 5 roads).

Rank of Nearest Road

	Vandalized	Unvandalized	
Rank 3	6 (35%)	11 (65%)	17
Rank 4	25 (54%)	21 (46%)	46
Rank 5	9 (28%)	23 (72%)	32
	40	55	95

$$x^2 = 5.74 \qquad df = 2 \qquad p < .10$$

In summary, late sites with masonry architecture located over 20 miles from the nearest town and within 100 m of a dirt road would appear to be the most vulnerable to vandalism, based on the results of the Sacred Mountain class II survey.

2. Previously recorded sites (BLM site files)

The numerous previously recorded sites exhibit a similar pattern of vandalism with respect to distance to nearest road. There was, however, no significant difference between vandalized or unvandalized sites on the basis of rank of nearest road or distance to nearest town.

Distance to Roads

	$\leq$100 m	101-400 m	401-800 m	0.8-1.6 km	over 1.6 km	
Vandalized	83 (51%)	42 (33%)	27 (26%)	37 (29%)	16 (28%)	205 (35%)
Unvandalized	79 (49%)	85 (67%)	78 (74%)	90 (71%)	41 (72%)	373 (65%)
	162	127	105	127	57	578

$$x^2 = 25.72 \qquad df = 4 \qquad p < .001$$

Distance to Nearest Town

	0-8 km	9-16 km	17-24 km	25-32 km	over 33 km	
Vandalized	11 (31%)	62 (36%)	47 (43%)	58 (33%)	27 (33%)	205 (35%)
Unvandalized	24 (69%)	112 (64%)	63 (57%)	120 (67%)	56 (67%)	375 (65%)
	35	174	110	178	83	580

$$x^2 = 3.73 \qquad df = 4 \qquad p < 0.50$$

59

Rank of Nearest Road

	2	3	4	5	
Vandalized	26 (36%)	37 (47%)	97 (33%)	44 (33%)	204 (35%)
Unvandalized	46 (64%)	42 (53%)	195 (67%)	89 (67%)	372 (65%)
	72	79	292	133	576

$$x^2 = 5.43 \qquad df = 3 \qquad p < 0.20$$

Other variables

During compilation of the various data categories, certain other variables were measured which were considered to be of importance to the problem of vandalism. In general, these data are not as complete as the other variables and the results should be considered as limited or tentative. Three questions were considered: 1) Is there a tendency for sites marked on U.S.G.S. topographic maps as ruins to be vandalized, in other words, are these maps being used to locate sites?; 2) Are sites exposed by pinyon-juniper chaining activities being potted more heavily than those in other locations?; and 3) Among architectural sites, what areas of the sites are being vandalized?

With regard to the first question, no sites which were formally noted on maps were recorded by the class II inventory. Twenty-eight previously recorded sites are on maps, and 18 (64%) have been vandalized by illegal digging. This percentage is about twice that of vandalized sites in the total sample, but we feel more research should be done on this factor before a relationship is established between sites noted on maps and incidence of vandalism.

It appears that pinyon-juniper chaining, which exposes sites, does not lead to increased vandalism according to the following figures:

Data source	Total sites recorded in chained areas	Total vandalized	Total unvandalized
Class II inventory	17	1 (6%)	16 (94%)
BLM site files	96	26 (27%)	70 (73%)
TOTALS	113	27 (24%)	86 (76%)

This distribution might be anticipated, however, since although chaining exposes sites, it also removes tree cover which serves to hide the illegal activities. In other words, working in open, chained areas also exposes the vandal to detection.

In order to determine the areas within architectural site boundaries being vandalized, counts were made for the class II inventory sites and those in the BLM site file of potting in either the roomblocks (rubble mounds) or the midden areas. No instances of digging in kivas were noted in either case. These results are as follows:

Data source	Total architectural sites	Roomblock vandalized	Midden vandalized	Undetermined (not recorded)
Class II inventory	29	11 (38%)	18 (62%)	0
BLM site files	178	41 (23%)	79 (44%)	58 (33%)
TOTALS	207	52 (25%)	97 (47%)	58 (28%)

Thus, the totals indicate that approximately twice as much digging takes place in the middens as in roomblocks. This is to be expected since relatively easier digging can be found in the trash deposits; furthermore, burials with ceramic accompaniments are commonly located in these areas. At architectural sites, only ten cases were noted to have potting in both the midden and roomblocks. However, it should be observed that these figures do not reflect the whole picture since the middens are frequently more heavily dug in than the rooms. Good data on this subject are not available for the previously recorded sites since rarely were the number of extant potholes reported. At one site recorded during the class II inventory, the midden contained over 43 discernible holes, and two others had more than 15 separate holes in evidence.

Field Implementation

A field check of previously recorded archaeological sites was conducted to provide supplementary data for making objective estimates of the nature and type of vandalism occurring on cultural resource sites within southwestern Colorado. In order to standardize on-site observations and provide a data base adequate for quantification, a preliminary version of a vandalism recording form was drafted prior to the beginning of fieldwork; Appendix A gives a completed example of this preliminary version. Minor changes were found to be necessary in this form and Appendix B exhibits the final recommended version. This vandalism form is intended to accompany the State of Colorado Archaeological Site form.

A sample of 81 archaeological sites was selected from the total population of unvandalized sites in the study area. This sample was chosen so that the major temporal periods of the Pueblo Tradition and the dates of recording would be adequately represented. The results of this selection process are given in Table 1. Temporally indeterminate petroglyph sites were also included in the sample.

Table 1. Selection of sites according to temporal period and date of recording.

Temporal Period	Date of Recording		Total
	Pre-1970	Post-1970	
Basketmaker III	18 (37) (72)	7 (22) (28)	25 (31) (100)
Pueblo I-Pueblo II	12 (24) (67)	6 (19) (33)	18 (22) (100)
Pueblo II-Pueblo III	17 (35) (47)	19 (59) (53)	36 (44) (100)
Petroglyphs	2 (4) (100)	0 --- ---	2 (2) (100)
TOTAL	49 (100) (60)	32 (100) (40)	81

Key: 18 = frequency
(37) = column percentage
(72) = row percentage

62

The date of site recording was included as a major category in an effort to assess the recency of site vandalism. Originally, three recording periods were formulated: 1965-1970, 1971-1975, and 1976-1980, but that scheme was found to be inoperative due to the limited number of sites recorded in the 1971-1975 time period. These three groupings subsequently were collapsed into the two broader categories of sites recorded prior to 1970 and those recorded after 1970.

It was intended at the outset that at least 60 sites--10 sites for each of the six categories--would need to be located so that an accurate assessment of vandalism could be made. An additional 21 sites were included in the sample to allow for the probability that the fieldworkers might not be able to locate all of the sites.

Selection of the particular sites to fill the six "cells" was done on a somewhat random basis, rejection of many of the sites occurring if a site was located more than a mile from any access, if access was particularly difficult, or if the site description was notably brief. It can be seen in Table 1 that representation within each cell and for each category is uneven, noticeably so in the post-1970 BMIII and PI-PII cells which fall short of the desired 10 sites, and the substantial majority of pre-1970 sites compared to post-1970 sites. A better, but certainly not ideal, sampling of sites for prehistoric temporal periods was attained.

Fieldwork and Relocation Strategy

All of the sites selected in the sample were plotted on U.S.G.S. topographic quadrangles according to their established locations on the map files maintained by the BLM, Montrose District. Aerial photographs obtained from the Colorado Geological Survey that correspond to each of the topographic maps were employed to gain a better understanding of local terrain and to identify access routes. The aerial photos proved to be an invaluable aid, especially in more remote parts of the study area.

Actual relocation of the sites was accomplished by a two-person crew during two successive time periods: June 16 to June 24, 1980, and July 4 to July 14, 1980. A total of 272 person-hours was spent in completing the field check portion of the study.

Using the topographic quadrangles, the aerial photos, and location descriptions recorded on the original site forms, an attempt was made to locate each site. Efforts were made to drive as close to the site as possible so that walking time could be minimized. Use of a four-wheel drive vehicle greatly enhanced the ability of the crew to get within reasonable walking distance of a site. Once the immediate vicinity of the site was reached by vehicle, an intensive reconnaissance of the area was undertaken using prominent topographic features for orientation. In ideal situations, the terrain was distinct or was described accurately enough that the site could be quickly relocated. In many cases, however, more extensive coverage was necessary because a description was vague and/or the site could not be immediately relocated. The maximum amount of time spent in relocating a site was approximately one hour. If, by the end of that hour, the site had not been found, further reconnaissance was suspended and the site was recorded as being "Not Found."

Relocation Results

From the original sample of 81 sites, a total of 61 sites was relocated. Of those 61 sites, 20 were found to have been vandalized; 41 showed no indications of vandalism. A breakdown of the 61 sites according to the two previously established categories of temporal period and recording date is given in Tables 2, 3, and 4.

As Table 2 indicates, a good balance was achieved between the relocation of those sites recorded prior to 1970 and those recorded after 1970, the numbers of pre-1970 sites being only slightly greater. Such a balance, however, was not attained for the temporal periods: approximately equal numbers of PI-PII and PII-PIII sites were relocated (22 and 23, respectively), but a somewhat smaller number of BMIII sites was found (15 sites).

Tables 3 and 4 were constructed to determine whether observable relationships existed between vandalized and unvandalized sites, respectively, and the temporal periods and recording dates. A subjective interpretation of Tables 3 and 4 indicates that greater numbers of BMIII and PI-PII sites recorded prior to 1970 have been vandalized than sites of those periods recorded after 1970; equal numbers of PII-PIII sites have been vandalized whether they were recorded before or after 1970. For unvandalized sites the situation is reversed, however: as many pre-1970 as post-1970 sites for the BMIII and PI-PII periods have not been disturbed. It is more likely for PII-PIII sites recorded after 1970 not to be disturbed.

Does a statistically significant relationship exist between the categories of temporal period and recording date and the presence of vandalism? Or, to state it somewhat differently: are sites of particular temporal periods more likely to have been vandalized if they were recorded prior to or after 1970? To answer those questions a simple chi-square test was performed on both Tables 3 and 4. In both cases, the results of the chi-square test were not significant. There is a good possibility, however, that the sample size has affected the results of the chi-square and, hence, we should not reject prematurely such a possibility.

Table 2. Breakdown of all located sites according to temporal period and recording date.

| Temporal Period | Date of Recording | | Total |
	Pre-1970	Post-1970	
Basketmaker III	9 (28) (60)	6 (21) (40)	15 (25) (100)
Pueblo I-Pueblo II	13 (41) (59)	9 (31) (41)	22 (36) (100)
Pueblo II-Pueblo III	9 (28) (39)	14 (48) (61)	23 (38) (100)
Petroglyphs	1 (3) (100)	0 --- ---	1 (2) (100)
TOTAL	32 (100) (52)	29 (100) (48)	61

Key: 9 = frequency
(28) = column percentage
(60) = row percentage

65

Table 3. Breakdown of vandalized sites according
to temporal period and recording date.

| Temporal Period | Date of Recording | | Total |
	Pre-1970	Post-1970	
Basketmaker III	4 (29) (80)	1 (17) (20)	5 (25) (100)
Pueblo I-Pueblo II	5 (36) (83)	1 (17) (17)	6 (30) (100)
Pueblo II-Pueblo III	4 (29) (50)	4 (67) (50)	8 (40) (100)
Petroglyphs	1 (7) (100)	0 --- ---	1 (5) (100)
TOTAL	14 (101) (70)	6 (101) (30)	20

Key: 4   = frequency
     (29) = column percentage
     (80) = row percentage

Table 4. Breakdown of unvandalized sites according
to temporal period and recording date.

| Temporal Period | Date of Recording | | Total |
	Pre-1970	Post-1970	
Basketmaker III	5 (28) (50)	5 (22) (50)	10 (24) (100)
Pueblo I-Pueblo II	8 (44) (50)	8 (35) (50)	16 (39) (100)
Pueblo II-Pueblo III	5 (28) (33)	10 (43) (67)	15 (37) (100)
TOTAL	18 (100) (44)	23 (100) (56)	41

Key: 5   = frequency
     (28) = column percentage
     (50) = row percentage

Data Manipulations

Site and Spatial Characteristics

As was mentioned in the introduction, one of the primary goals
of the field check portion of the study was to test a vandalism
recording form. This form was designed so that, once the results were
compiled, those physical characteristics that significantly influenced
the likelihood of site vandalism could be isolated. In this portion
of the analysis, attention is focused upon those categories incorporated
within Section II (Site Characteristics) and Section IV (Spatial
Characteristics) of the form.

Appendix C presents a compilation of specified characteristics for
each relocated site. This form tabulates, in addition to site number
and presence of vandalism, the type and period of the site (under the
general heading of Site Characteristics), the distance to the nearest
road and the rank of that road, the distance to the nearest community
and the size of that community, and the distance to the nearest intrusion and the type of intrusion (the latter three categories subsumed
under the general heading of Spatial Characteristics).

Table 5 presents, in summary fashion, the frequency and percentage
of those categories other than presence of vandalism and temporal period
(previously summarized in Tables 2, 3, and 4). Figure 21 is a graphic
reformulation of Table 5. Table 5 and Figure 21 demonstrate that the
typical relocated site possesses architecture, pottery, and lithics;
is closer to a jeep road; located nearer to a community of less than
100; and situated in the vicinity of an agricultural field, residence,
or chained area.

The question still remains of whether there exists a demonstrable
and significant relationship between the occurrence of vandalism and the
physical and spatial characteristics of a site. In descriptive fashion,
we can first compare the spatial characteristics of all sites with the
vandalized sites.

Table 5. Summary statistics for categories site type, road rank, size of nearest community, and type of nearest intrusion.

Category code/label	Frequency	Percentage
Architectural Site		
1 yes	49	81.7
2 no	11	18.3
Lithic Site		
1 yes	51	85.0
2 no	9	15.0
Pottery Site		
1 yes	56	93.3
2 no	4	6.7
Rockshelter Site		
1 yes	5	8.3
2 no	55	91.7
Hearth Site		
1 yes	1	1.7
2 no	59	98.3
Cist Site		
1 yes	6	10.0
2 no	54	90.0
Road Rank		
2 all weather	11	18.3
3 seasonal use	14	23.3
4 jeep road	34	56.7
5 trail	1	1.7
Size of Community		
1 less than 100	35	58.3
3 501-1000	9	15.0
5 greater than 5000	16	26.7
Type of Intrusion		
0 NA	14	23.3
1 field	13	21.7
2 well	1	1.7
3 reservoir	2	3.3
4 residence	10	16.7
6 chained area	7	11.7
7 other	13	21.7

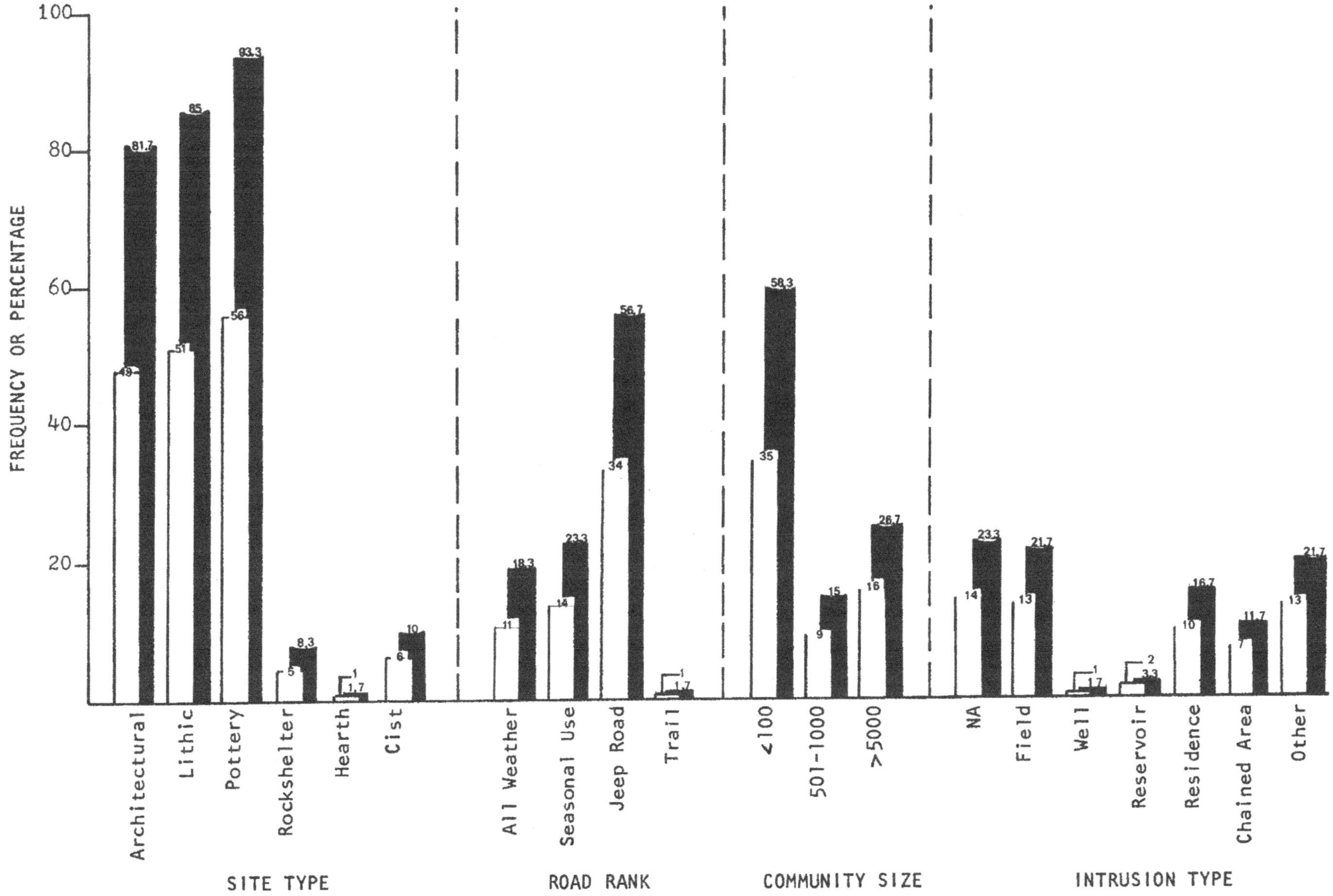

Figure 21. Frequency (white) and percentage (black) of Site and Spatial Characteristics of relocated sites. Actual values of sub-categories indicated.

69

Table 6. Spatial characteristics of all sites compared to vandalized sites.

| Variable | All Sites (N=61) | | | Vandalized Sites (N=20) | | |
| | Range | | Mean | Range | | Mean |
	Min	Max		Min	Max	
Distance to nearest road	0	1613	338.1	0	645	145.6
Distance to nearest community	2.7	51.3	20.4	4.2	34.0	18.8
Distance to nearest intrusion	0	5160	869.7	0	800	160.5

Table 6 suggests that vandalized sites are located, on the average, closer to roads, communities, and intrusions. A Student's t test was performed to ascertain whether the observed measurements on the three variables for the vandalized sites differed significantly from those of the entire sample. T-values of 2.18, 0.62, and 1.64 were obtained for the distance to nearest road, community, and intrusion variables, respectively. Only one of those t-values--distance to nearest road--was found to be significant $(.05 \geq p \geq .02)$.

Patterns in the data are beginning to emerge. Continuing in an exploratory fashion, the statistical technique of multiple regression was employed to determine if the presence of vandalism on a site could be explained or predicted by that site's physical or spatial characteristics. In other words, to what degree can the variation in the dependent variable (Presence of Vandalism) be explained by the variation in the independent variables (Site Characteristics and Spatial Characteristics) considered individually or combinatorially?

The SPSS subprogram REGRESSION was utilized to discover possible relationships between the dependent variable and the independent variables. In the first procedure, the dependent variable Presence of Vandalism was regressed against the independent variables, the six categories of Spatial Characteristics. Results of this first procedure are displayed in Table 7. At the top, the table lists the independent variables in the order of their ability to explain the variation in the

Table 7. Multiple regression on variables of vandalism study l.

DEPENDENT VARIABLE.. VAR02 PRESENCE OF VANDALISM

VARIABLE(S) ENTERED ON STEP NUMBER 1...

VAR13	DISTANCE TO NEAREST ROAD, IN METERS
VAR18	TYPE OF NEAREST INTRUSION
VAR16	SIZE OF NEAREST COMMUNITY
VAR14	RANK OF NEAREST ROAD
VAR17	DISTANCE TO NEAREST INTRUSION, IN METERS
VAR15	DISTANCE TO NEAREST COMMUNITY, IN KILOME

MULTIPLE R	.41874	SUM OF SQUARES	MEAN SQUARE
R SQUARE	.17535	2.33796	.38986
ADJUSTED R SQUARE	.08199	10.99537	.20746
STD DEVIATION	.45548		

F 1.87824   SIGNIFICANCE .102

SUMMARY TABLE

VARIABLE ENTERED	F TO ENTER	SIGNIFICANCE	MULTIPLE R	R SQUARE	R SQUARE CHANGE	SIMPLE R	OVERALL F	SIGNIFICANCE
VAR13	3.98635	.051	.36076	.13015	.13015	.36076	1.87824	.102
VAR18	.18684	.667	.36899	.13616	.00601	-.08116		
VAR16	.35233	.555	.37955	.14406	.00790	-.08671		
VAR14	.87740	.353	.38470	.14799	.00394	-.07348		
VAR17	1.45933	.232	.41333	.17084	.02285	.26506		
VAR15	.28953	.593	.41874	.17535	.00450	.11040		

71

dependent variable; the R Square value below that indicates the strength of the relationship. The test of significance of this relationship is reflected in the F ratio and the corresponding probability of that F ratio. This F ratio is referred to as an "overall" test for goodness of fit of the regression equation: it indicates "whether the (assumed random) sample of observations being analyzed has been drawn from a population in which the multiple correlation is equal to zero" (Kim and Kohout 1975:335). In this example, variables of all six Spatial Characteristics combine to explain 17.5% of the variation in the dependent variable, Presence of Vandalism. The F ratio is 1.88, and the probability of getting a ratio equal to or greater than 1.88 is slightly greater than 10%.

At the bottom of Table 7 is a Summary Table which clarifies the contributions of the individual independent variables. In this particular case only one variable, distance to nearest road, is consequential: it contributes approximately 13% of the variation in the dependent variable and has an F ratio of 3.99 which is significant at slightly more than .05. The other five variables make significantly weaker contributions. It is interesting to note, however, that once the effects of the preceding variables have been removed, distance to nearest intrusion has a greater, although not statistically significant, effect on the dependent variable.

Table 8 shows the effects of the eight independent variables of Site Characteristics upon the dependent variable. The results of this procedure are substantially poorer than those obtained from the Spatial Characteristics, but may be examined for heuristic purposes. Considered together, the eight independent variables contribute only 10.9% of the variation in the dependent variable. The F ratio is .782 with a probability of .621, thus making it more likely that the observed multiple correlation is due to sampling fluctuation or measurement error. It is provocative that the presence of architecture on a site makes a greater contribution, in terms of the other independent variables, to the variation in the dependent variable. This is certainly not a surprising revelation and it does make intuitive sense. It is reassuring, however, that such

Table 8. Multiple regression on variables of vandalism study II.

DEPENDENT VARIABLE.. VAR02   PRESENCE OF VANDALISM

VARIABLE(S) ENTERED ON STEP NUMBER   1..

VAR03	ARCHITECTURAL SITE
VAR05	POTTERY SITE
VAR11	PUEBLO 1-PUEBLO 2
VAR07	HEARTH SITE
VAR06	ROCKSHELTER SITE
VAR08	CIST SITE
VAR04	LITHIC SITE
VAR10	BASKETMAKER 3

MULTIPLE R	.33047	SUM OF SQUARES	MEAN SQUARE	F SIGNIFICANCE
R SQUARE	.10921	1.45617	.18202	.78159 .621
ADJUSTED R SQUARE	0	11.87716	.23289	
STD DEVIATION	.48258			

S U M M A R Y   T A B L E

VARIABLE ENTERED	F TO ENTER	SIGNIFICANCE	MULTIPLE R	R SQUARE	R SQUARE CHANGE	SIMPLE R	OVERALL F	SIGNIFICANCE
VAR03	2.54213	.117	.24366	.05937	.05937	.24366	.78159	.621
VAR05	.15671	.694	.24631	.06067	.00130	-.04725		
VAR11	.10413	.748	.27885	.07775	.01708	-.09782		
VAR07	.17467	.678	.28165	.07933	.00157	-.09206		
VAR06	1.02790	.315	.30582	.09352	.01419	-.17056		
VAR08	.33648	.564	.31065	.09650	.00298	-.11785		
VAR04	.00062	.977	.31070	.09653	.00003	0		
VAR10	.72591	.398	.33047	.10921	.01268	0		

intuitively recognized relationships are supported by the more
objective, statistical methods. Here again, it can be seen that a
second variable, rockshelter site, is elevated to a significance
slightly greater than its counterparts when the preceding variables
are removed from the equation.

Nature of Vandalism

The Vandalism Recording Form (see Appendix B) is constructed so
as to record for each vandalized site the nature of vandalism in addition
to the physical and spatial characteristics. This section is included
in order to obtain a more comprehensive, standardized, and objective
evaluation of the how, where, and extensiveness of site vandalism.
Table 9 summarizes succinctly for each vandalized site the location of
disturbance, method of disturbance, and intensity of disturbance, as well
as making recommendations for ameliorating the effects of the vandalism.
Table 10 is a synthesis of values recorded in two of the categories in
Table 9. For the category intensity of disturbance, the recorded values
ranged from a minimum of 1 percent to a maximum of 75 percent, with a
mean of 24.7 percent.

It would appear that when a site is disturbed, vandals typically
explore the roomblock and midden of a site, a shovel being their preferred instrument of disturbance, and succeed, on the average, in disturbing approximately one-quarter of the site.

As mentioned earlier, specific recommendations to rectify damage
have been formulated for each damaged site. More general recommendations for counteracting vandalistic activities, utilizing the data
gathered in this study, are proposed in the final chapter. Before
proceeding, however, it might be instructive to compare the results of
this study with a more informal one conducted in the same general area.

Comparisons

Between August 19 and October 11, 1975, an evaluation of the
necessity of stabilization of archaeological ruins in the (then) proposed
Sand Canyon Archaeological Lands was conducted at the request of the BLM
by the University of Colorado Mesa Verde Research Center, under the

Table 9. Nature and extent of vandalism on all vandalized sites.

SITE NO.	LOCATION OF DISTURBANCE[1]	METHOD OF DISTURBANCE[2]	INTENSITY OF DISTURBANCE[3]	RECOMMENDATIONS
5MT137	1, 2, 3	3, 4	50	Excavate & stabilize disturbed area; reroute road
5MT275	2, 5	1	1	Excavate trash midden to recover remainder of burial
5MT1580	2, 4	1	75	Excavate potholes; stabilize slab cists
5MT1595	1, 2, 3, 6, 7	1, 8	10	Excavate potholes; stabilize walls; backfill midden
5MT1602	2	3, 4	5	Reroute or close road
5MT1643	1, 2	3	10	Excavate entire site
5MT1667	1, 2	4	10	Excavate disturbed area; reroute road
5MT1841	1	1	25	Excavate pothole; remove initials from lintel
5MT1850	1	1	40	Excavate pothole
5MT1852	1	1	5	Excavate potholes; remove trash
5MT1960	1	1	25	Excavate pothole & stabilize tower walls
5MT2021	1, 2	4	10	Excavate disturbed area; reroute road
5MT2107	1, 3	1, 2	50	Backfill excavated areas; close road; remove trash
5MT2123	1	4	70	Excavate site; determine nature of historic component
5MT2137	1, 2	1	1	Excavate potholes; remove fence
5MT2636	1	1, 8	1	Excavate pothole
5MT4044	2	3	50	Excavate midden area
5MT4085	1, 3	1	10	Excavate site and stabilize walls
5MT4352	1, 2	1	20	Excavate potholes
5MT4575	1	4	1	Close roads; remove garbage
5MT303	7	8	50	Remove recent graffiti if possible; construct protective fence around site

[1]Location: 1=roomblock, 2=midden, 3=pit structure, 4=cist, 5=burial, 6=rockshelter, 7=rock wall

[2]Method: 1=shovel, 2=screen, 3=chain, 4=blade, 5=backhoe, 6=dynamite, 7=bullets, 8=graffiti

[3]Percentage of total site extent

Table 10. Synthesis of factors of disturbance.

Category	Frequency[1]	Percentage of Vandalized Sites
LOCATION OF DISTURBANCE		
Roomblock	16	76
Midden	11	52
Pit Structure	4	19
Cist	1	5
Burial	1	5
Rockshelter	1	5
Rock Wall	1	5
METHOD OF DISTURBANCE		
Shovel	12	57
Screen	1	5
Chain	4	19
Blade	6	29
Backhoe	0	0
Dynamite	0	0
Bullets	0	0
Graffiti	3	14

[1]Total for each of the two categories should exceed 20 since some of the sites had more than one location or method of disturbance.

direction of Dr. David A. Breternitz. Fieldwork supervision and completion of the final report were conducted by Curtis W. Martin. As described by Martin (1976:2),

> The field work consisted of visiting each previously recorded site in the project area. Detailed descriptions of each visible structure and its stabilization requirements were made, the area of the site requiring stabilization work was photographed, and a map of each site was constructed.

Stabilization forms were completed on 42 previously recorded sites. In addition, 7 previously unrecorded sites were encountered during the course of the fieldwork and were subsequently recorded on archaeological inventory, as well as stabilization, forms.

In addition to detailed recommendations concerning stabilization requirements, comments on the present site condition (including descriptions of both natural disturbance and vandalism), amount of disturbance recognized since the original recording, and distance to roads/trails were made. On a general level, Martin (1976:3) describes the occurrence of site vandalism for this group of sites:

> A significant amount of vandalism and natural weathering has occurred at almost all of the sites, and, as evidenced by the amount of each which has occurred since the sites were recorded in the latter half of the 1960's, is continuing to take place.

He goes on to recount particularly noticeable incidences of site vandalism.

Of the 49 sites that were evaluated, Martin found that 35 (71%) of those sites had been vandalized in some way. This vandalism consisted generally of digging in roomblocks or pit structures, destruction of walls, carving of names, initials, or dates into walls, and even dynamiting. In terms of the recency of the vandalism, disturbance had occurred since the original surveys (1965 and 1968) on 13 (33%) of the 33 vandalized sites. On the new sites that Martin recorded, 2 (29%) of those 7 had been vandalized.

Appendix D contains a compilation of all the previously recorded sites that Martin evaluated and for which quantitative information comparable to the present study is available. Summary statistics for all of the sites and the vandalized sites considered alone are presented along with the Appendix. These results indicate that a large percentage of the sites are vandalized, PII-PIII in age, and located at an average of 305 meters from the nearest road, 31.1 kilometers from the nearest community, and 1557 meters from the nearest intrusion. Although site type was not incorporated into this compilation since the Sand Canyon data is not as complete as that of the present study, Martin (1976) did record the general site type and the number of visible rooms/features. Out of the 49 sites, 31 (63%) of them were recorded as cliff dwellings; the remainder were masonry structures under rockshelters or surface rubble. The number of rooms/features on a cliff dwelling site ranged from 1-10, the average being 3.7 rooms/features per site; the other sites averaged 2.2 rooms/features per site.

The summary statistics at the bottom in Appendix D can be compared to those compiled in Table 6. In contrast to the present study, the mean distances for the Sand Canyon sites are approximately equivalent between all sites and the vandalized sites; in fact, the distance to the nearest intrusion for the vandalized sites is greater than that for all sites. The mean distances to roads, communities, and intrusions for the Sand Canyon sites are substantially larger than those recorded in the present study.

The most likely explanation of the discrepancies between these two data sets lies, we believe, in the nature of the surrounding terrain and that of the sites themselves. The sites relocated during the present study tend for the most part to be located in pinyon-juniper woodlands and do not possess overly distinctive architectural features. These two factors combine to decrease the visibility--and, hence, the potential destruction-- of these sites. The majority of the Sand Canyon sites, on the other hand, are highly visible cliff dwellings with multiple architectural features located usually under overhangs in steep-walled sandstone canyons where vegetation is sparser. Martin (1976) observes, in fact, that many of these sites are visible from roads. Thus, despite their greater distances from modern intrusions, the Sand Canyon sites are more readily visible to even the most amateur of vandals and offer greater possibilities for obtaining artifacts.

Summary

The data presented in this chapter confirm what has been
generally believed regarding characteristics of archaeological sites
and incidences of vandalism. There can be no doubt that variables
such as the type and age of a prehistoric site, along with relatively
easy access routes, are critical to the vandal's activities. On the
other hand, the figures given for the various data categories are also
important in and of themselves since they represent quantitative
definition of the overall problem. Although there is considerable room
for future refinement of the data, it may be observed that the foregoing
figures are the first to be tabulated which serve to reflect the overall
seriousness of the problem and how widespread it has become over the
years. There is one extremely important factor associated with the
vandalism problem which cannot be accurately judged by reviewing the
known site data or collecting additional field information. This is,
of course, the human aspect of the problem, a topic which is examined
in the next chapter.

V

DATA PRESENTATION: INFORMANT INTERVIEWS

General

This portion of the study was designed to find out about habits of local people who are interested in archaeology and have dug or collected artifacts. Specifically, we wanted information about who is digging, what has been collected, when and from where, how much time was spent, what kinds of sites people prefer, and how they became interested in digging and collecting. Attitudes about archaeology, archaeologists, the government, and preservation in general were also sought.

Past studies (Williams 1977; Rippeteau 1979; Scott 1977) have focused on cultural resource managers' opinions of how people dig and surface collect. This study attempts an "emic" perspective by asking local informants to describe their habits, motives and feelings.

The emic/etic distinction is relevant. According to Harris (1968:574), emic studies are "concerned with the analysis of the behavior stream in terms of the intentions, purposes, motives, goals, attitudes, thoughts and feelings of the culture carriers." In contrast, "etic statements depend upon phenomenal distinctions judged appropriate by the community of scientific observers" (Harris 1968:575). This study falls within the bounds of traditional ethnography in its dependence upon information offered by those belonging to the group being studied. Information solicited, however, was structured by a detailed list of topics to be explored.

The distinction between ideal behavior and actual behavior is also pertinent. This distinction is based on the assumption that "there is one set of patterned regularities consisting of what people say or believe about what they do or should do and another set of patterned regularities concerned with what they 'actually' do" (Harris 1968:580). It cannot be verified here whether the data accumulated represent ideal behavior or actual behavior. We can only analyze what the informants say they believe and what they say they do.

Method

We decided to interview local informants at length. We put together a long questionnaire for the interviewer to use as a guideline. Choice of topics to include was based on Williams' (1977) and Scott's (1977) summaries of factors that cultural resource managers believe to be important in site vandalism. Aside from government regulations prohibiting use of written questionnaires without prior Federal permission, we believed that more complete answers could be obtained by direct questioning than by asking informants to mail in what developed into a very long form. In person, unclear questions could be explained or elaborated. Avenues of questioning could be explored and pursued, expanded or shortened as the tempo of the interview dictated. New questions could be added; inappropriate questions could be deleted. On the other hand, informants may have been more honest about some questions had they been able to anonymously mail in their responses.

A seven-page questionnaire was written, and specific questions and answer possibilities were incorporated for ease in checking off answers as the interview proceeded. The questionnaire formed a basic framework to follow and it insured that a complete set of data was collected during each interview. Every effort was made to record comments and opinions not included on the questionnaire, and unanticipated answers and information were welcomed. The original form and modifications to it are presented as Appendix E. A shorter version was considered. However, all the questions seemed to be pertinent and the original length was retained. Wording of some questions did prove to be confusing and the presence of the interviewer was an asset in interpreting the meaning.

The sample

The sample was devised with the help of BLM San Juan Resource Area archaeologists, Dolores Project archaeologists, and local people known to the interviewer. Choice of people to interview was based on a reputed interest in collecting prehistoric artifacts or in local archaeology. As names were gathered, it became obvious that certain individuals and families appeared over and over again. This provided something of a cross-check for depth of interest and reputation as a collector. It also implies that not many people in the area express an open, active interest in archaeology, that the interest is family-oriented, that it revolves around collections, and that commercial dealing is not a prime motivating force among this group of people, not to say that commercial dealing does not occur in the area.

No specific effort was made to vary the composition of the sample by age, occupation, or sex. A further non-random effect was introduced by availability: only those who could be reached by telephone and who agreed after a short introductory statement to talk to the interviewer were chosen. This eliminated several potentially good sources who could not be reached. It also eliminated three sources who refused to be interviewed and may represent a hostile or more serious group of collectors (or dealers) not included in this study.

The geographical region to be covered was another limiting factor. All respondents are from the Cortez-Dove Creek area due to the distance involved in interviewing a sample from the entire Resource Area, which stretches from east of Durango to the Utah border. The Montelores area (Montezuma and Dolores Counties) is the geographic center of the vandalism "impact" area, so this constraint is not necessarily a disadvantage. We also concentrated on the Montelores area because winter and spring, when the interviews were scheduled, are seasons when farmers are most available, and many collectors are farmers. Time did not permit interviewing several likely sources in the Durango area. These people differ from Montelores area collectors. Their interest seems to be directly tied to archaeology in itself and their professions do not draw them to the high site density areas. Cortez area residents, on the other hand, often develop an interest through continual exposure to Indian ruins, for example, in farming or energy exploration activities.

Interview techniques

Typically, the interviewer telephoned the informant and stated that she was conducting a survey of local people's attitudes and opinions on a variety of topics having to do with archaeology, archaeologists, and Indian ruins, for a private company. She asked if the informant would talk to her for one and a half to two hours, then set up an appointment for an interview at the convenience of the informant. Informants sometimes asked: 1) how their names were chosen; and 2) why the study was being done and if the information was going to the government. In answer, they were told that: 1) they were locally known to have an interest in archaeology; and 2) the study was being done by contract with BLM in order to help them manage Indian ruins on government land. No deception was involved at any time during the interview process, although the above information plus the interviewer's occupation as an archaeologist was not divulged unless specifically asked about.

Before the interview began, the informants were told that all their answers were confidential and their names would not be used. They were also asked to tell the interviewer if they did not wish to answer any question. Finally, they were told to view the interviewer as neutral, i.e., as not having an opinion on any of the questions asked.

The interviewer then went through the entire questionnaire, also recording comments and opinions that came up in the course of the answers. The questionnaire often provoked considerable comment and strong opinions among the informants, and the "opinion" questions were helpful in relaxing informants enough to talk about specific digging activities. Most people were willing to answer all questions. Some evasiveness or defensiveness was noted, but much less than had been expected, considering that all informants knew that some of the questions tended to be incriminating.

Usually at least two informants were present, often a husband and wife or other family members. The interviewer tried to make the experience amiable and comfortable, yet businesslike, and encouraged the informants to answer completely and to express all feelings or thoughts they might have.

At the end of the interview, the conversation often returned to subjects of interest on the questionnaire. Most informants were eager to show the interviewer their collections. Occasionally, some distrust of the whole experience was expressed, as though any information given to the government was likely to be used for purposes adverse to the interests of the informants. After the interview, additional impressions and notes were recorded.

A maximum of four interviews were conducted per day. The initial contacting process was extremely time consuming, with sometimes as many as four telephone calls necessary before an interview appointment could be made. Driving time was also a factor to be reckoned with. Twice, appointments were broken by informants who were not home at the time of the interview. To fill in at times when interviews could not be scheduled or fell through, the interviewer visited local artifact dealers, the Sheriff's Department, Ed and Jo Berger of Crow Canyon School (who sponsored a successful lecture series on Anasazi archaeology during the summer of 1979), and other local information sources.

Data compilation

Data were tallied by questionnaire answers and results are presented throughout the text. Results are tallied by individual answers (n-30) or by complete interview (n-20) depending on the nature of the question and on the amount of disagreement between individuals during the same interview. On some questions, multiple answers were possible; this is noted when it occurs. On other questions, people offered information about activities engaged in by friends or relatives, although they did not participate themselves. Since the sample is not statistically valid and is also quite small, results are expressed only as tallies or percentages. Percentages are rounded off to nearest tenths or whole numbers, so may not add up to 100%.

Although these results offer a summary of the interviews in a quantified format, feelings, mood, and qualitative aspects of the interviews are at least as relevant. The following discussion of results will incorporate both qualitative and quantitative aspects of the survey.

Results

Characteristics of the sample

The sample is characterized by its small size, long-term residence, old age, and limited geographic residence area. The small size is a result of the decision to interview in depth, which favors both quantity and quality of information per interview over quantity of interviews. Thirty individuals representing 20 separate interviews constitute the sample. Of these, 18 are men and 12 are women; 9 couples are included. Twenty-eight of the informants are married; two are single men. The sample is composed predominantly of the over-30 age group, and 10 of 20 interviews reported eldest children over 20 years old. Five individuals interviewed were under 30. Of the remaining, ten were in the 30 to 50 age bracket; fifteen were over 50.

People interviewed have lived in the Montelores area for a long time: a mean of 40.7 years. Nineteen have lived in the area all their lives and nine are third generation (or more) residents. Only one has lived in the area less than five years; two more have lived in the area less than 20 years.

Of those interviewed (by family), ten are farmers; two are construction workers; three are involved in drilling and oil exploration; three run small businesses; and two are federal employees. These occupations represent the major sources of income in the immediate area with the exception of cattle and sheep ranching, but the representation may not be proportional.

Informants' residences are scattered throughout the extensive area of Montezuma and Dolores Counties, as shown in Table 11. Four of twenty live in towns.

Table 11. Nearest community to informants' residence.

community	# informants (n-20)	%
Cortez	9	45%
Dolores	3	15%
Yellow Jacket	3	15%
Pleasant View	2	10%
Dove Creek	1	5%
Mancos	2	10%

Thirteen of 20 informants reported activity in local organizations such as grange, lodges, or community clubs, or held local public office. This indicates that the sample is well-established and well-known in the community. With the exception of two informants, the sample constitutes a group of people with long ties and a deep commitment to the Montelores area, as well as a long memory of the area's past and an awareness of increasingly rapid changes.

Taking into account the natural beauty, resources, and recreational potential of the area, it is not surprising that the sample reports a strong interest in camping, hunting, fishing, and picnicking (Table 12). Half are rockhounds. One-fourth are boaters and recreational 4-wheel drivers.

Table 12. Recreational activities of informants.*

activity	# informants (n-20)	% of total sample
recreational 4-wheel driving	5	25%
camping	17	85%
hunting	17	85%
fishing	19	95%
picnicking	19	95%
boating	5	25%
rockhounding	10	50%

*more than one answer possible

The sample expressed a strong interest in local history and archaeology (Table 13), also not surprising since this is partially the basis on which they were chosen. Aside from local ruins included in Table 14, fourteen reported visiting many other ruins in the Montelores area and in the greater Southwest, including Aztec, Navajo National Monument, Chaco Canyon, Salmon Ruin, and the Hopi Villages. Fourteen have visited ghost towns in the San Juans. However, most are more interested in the immediate Montelores area. Eighteen of twenty know about the Dolores Project display dig, and eight have visited it.

Table 13. Interest in local archaeology and history.

question	# interviews (n-30)			
	yes	%	no	%
Are you interested in local archaeology?	29	95.7%	1	3.3%
Are you interested in local history?	30	100.0%	0	.0%
Have you read any books on archaeology or local history?	26	85.8%	4	14.2%

Table 14. Local ruins visited.

ruin	# informants (n-20)	%
Mesa Verde National Park	20	100%
Hovenweep	19	95%
Escalante Ruin	17	85%
Lowry Ruins	19	95%

Of the people in the sample, all have collected prehistoric artifacts, nearly 75% have collected historic artifacts or dug for prehistoric artifacts, and many have moved ruin rubble, removed parts of structures, or dug for historic artifacts. Table 15 summarizes these activities.

Table 15. Participation in activities related to artifact hunting, digging, or sites

activity	# participating informants (n-20)	%
collecting prehistoric artifacts from the surface of the ground	20	100%
digging for prehistoric artifacts	14	70%
collecting historic artifacts from the surface of the ground	14	70%
digging for historic artifacts	8	40%
moving Indian ruin rubble (such as in clearing agricultural land)	13	65%
removing parts of structures (such as for obtaining barnwood or firewood)	6	30%

The people interviewed fall loosely into three groups: first, those with peripheral interest in the form of surface collecting; secondly, those with intense interest developed either through family ties or through close contact with high site density areas. These people are mostly farmers. A third group, more difficult to describe,

consists of those who are intensely interested in sites and may deal
in artifacts occasionally as a means of supplementing their collections
or their income. Commercial activity on a more serious level was thought
to occur by almost everybody and was known to some, but seems to be
either well hidden or is happening on a much smaller scale than was previously thought. Group 1 consists of individuals who, although some
have been exposed all their lives to ruins and artifact hunting, have
not developed a personal interest beyond picking up an arrowhead if
they chance to find one. This group probably describes most people who
live in the Montelores area. Some members of Group 1 are ethically
opposed to digging, and view it as site destruction. Group 2, on the
other hand, actively hunts for artifacts and often digs as well, and
uses such phrases as "It gets in your blood," and "It's not a hobby,
it's a love," to describe their feelings. Group 3 harbors a decreased
sentimental attachment to their "finds" through an interest level not
as specifically tied to artifacts or to family lands or experiences as
that of Group 2, and more specifically tied to the sites themselves
and to knowledge of prehistory.

Topics covered by the questionnaire are discussed below, and
differences between attitudes of the above groups are explored. The
term "pothunter" was not used in the questionnaire and is not used
below because it is emotionally loaded with negative connotations. In
its broadest applications, it includes many practicing archaeologists
in the state. In its narrowest applications, it includes only commercial
diggers. In any case, no purpose is served by referring to the people
interviewed as "pothunters."

Collections

Nineteen of 20 informants have collections; the twentieth has a
"family" collection at the parents' house. Decorated whole pots, mugs,
and arrowheads are prized items, but collections also include jewelry,
perishables, non-artifactual material such as bones and corn, ground
stone, bottles, sherds, and flakes. Collections range in size from
one small frame of arrowheads to over 2000 items (Table 16).

Table 16. Collection size.

# items	# informants (n-20)	%
no answer	2	10%
under 20	4	20%
20 - 50	4	20%
51 - 100	1	5%
101 - 500	6	30%
over 500	2	10%

Most collections are displayed in the home, some in elaborately designed, space-consuming display cases. Most consist of found items with only three informants of 20 reporting trading for items or buying items. Differences in the three groups described above become clear with the following comments concerning collections: A surface collector says, "We don't specifically hunt for anything, but we keep the things we find. If we didn't somebody else would pick them up." A collector says, "Our collection has been our lifetime. Each piece is a part of us." A person from Group 3, whose attitude most closely approximates that of archaeologists in many ways, says, "'Finds' are not important. Knowledge, enjoyment and getting out are the important parts of artifact collecting. Any find is a 'first-rate find.'" Table 17 summarizes these and other attitudes about collections.

Table 17. Attitudes about collections.

question	# informants (n-20)			
	yes	%	no	%
Do you place a dollar value on your collection?	2	10%	18	90%
Do you display your collection at home?	17	85%	3	15%
Have you ever donated any part of your collection to a museum?	5	25%	15	75%
Have you ever sold any artifacts you found?	2	10%	18	90%
Would the sale of your artifacts increase your interest in artifact hunting?	2	10%	18	90%

Of thirty informants, two report having sold artifacts; twenty-eight report that sale of artifacts would not increase their interest in artifact hunting--in fact, would decrease their interest. One farmer says, "I wouldn't sell at all. Artifacts wouldn't mean as much to people you sold them to. I feel I've saved rather than destroyed artifacts by caring for what I've plowed up. You couldn't live here without destroying Indian ruins." An elderly woman says, "The collection is to be left in the family. It is definitely not for sale. It's a family heirloom to be passed down to children and grandchildren." The many people with this attitude view their collections as tied to their own land or land which they consider to be a part of their family history, i.e., all of southwestern Colorado. Objects are associated as well with memories of family outings and get-togethers. The collection symbolizes the life histories of the family members. A past BLM ranger from the local area speculated that Dolores Archaeological Project artifacts have little meaning to local people for the same reason: they are not tied to family or personal experiences or land.

Five families have donated objects to museums. However, an ingrained distrust of museums was obvious among those in the sample. Museums are viewed as institutions that accept prized items which are never again seen by the donors. Informants report instances of museums losing items and are irritated when their objects are not displayed. Conversely, they are proud of objects displayed at the Mesa Verde Museum, the largest local showplace for privately owned items. One past donor says, "I frown on donating items to museums because after a while, nobody knows what's happened to them. Somebody hauls them off." Others say they would donate objects to a local museum if one was available. Still, many have a sense of ownership of their collection that transcends donation. Another man says:

> I would be interested in loaning to another museum, or would
> donate objects for display locally if a place was available.
> I know of a donation of pottery all from one fellow's burial--
> the museum split up the donation. They didn't see the value
> in keeping it all together. When you donate to a museum, or
> loan even, you may not get your objects back. You don't know
> what will happen to them. I would like to see my things
> displayed.

An archaeologist who has worked extensively in the area reports the attitude that artifacts ought to be out of the ground where people can enjoy them; that excludes museum storage. Some concern was expressed not only by informants but by archaeologists and museum professionals in the area that there is no local institution that has the storage, display space, or curatorial capabilities to accept collections belonging to local people, some of which are quite extensive. Collections are split and lost or sold piece by piece when elder family members die.

From a museum's perspective, collections that are merely on loan cannot be adequately managed; legal pitfalls are apt to occur and hard-to-come-by funds are very reluctantly spent on objects that the museum does not own. Except in rare open-storage museums, only a fraction of a museum's collections can usually be displayed at any one time. A question remains as to whether museum display of objects that may have been illegally obtained encourages digging.

A less common attitude describes the experience of finding as the central attractive quality of artifact hunting: "Once objects are found, they're just a bunch of objects with no special significance." Anyone who has ever found an artifact would be hard pressed to admit that the thrill of finding does not contribute to an interest in archaeology.

Most people know of a few individuals who have sold artifacts, but none who sell regularly. Selling artifacts is viewed as a form of supplementary income for some, and it has a long history of providing extra money, dating especially to Depression times but also to as far back as the Wetherill expeditions. One man recalls, "During the depression, a man from New York was paying $2 to $3 a pot or $5 a day for digging. The only professional diggers I ever knew worked for him. One fellow bought a place and paid for it with pots in the 20's or 30's." Another says, "We were out running cows and we found a caved-out bank with two pots eroding out of it. We were in college and hard up for cash, so we sold them." As times get difficult, an upsurge in artifact sales can be predicted. Buyers are described as easy to find, and informants cited frequent local newspaper classified ads for buyers, some of which were apparently placed by the BLM as a foil.

Table 18 presents data concerning knowledge of persons who sell artifacts.

Table 18. Sale of artifacts.

question	# informants			
	yes	%	no	%
Do you know others who have sold artifacts? (n-20)	14	70%	6	30%

	0	%	1-2	%	3-5	%	6-10	%	over 10	%	don't know	%
How many do you know? (n-20)	6	30%	6	30%	5	25%	1	5%	2	10%	0	0%
How many sell regularly? (n-14)	8	56.8%	2	14.2%	3	21.3%	0	0%	0	0%	1	7.1%

Of those who knew of artifact sales, seven reported out-of-state
buyers, two reported out-of-town buyers, and two reported local buyers.
Six stated that they knew people who buy and resell artifacts (Table 19).
Whole decorated vessels and mugs are known to sell best. No informants
said they specifically looked for certain objects to sell. One man said
with disdain, "What sells best? Anything anybody can put in their home
and show off."

Table 19. Knowledge of artifact dealers.

question	# informants (n-20)					
	yes	%	no	%	don't know	%
Do you know people who buy and resell prehistoric artifacts?	6	30%	14	70%	0	0
Is it difficult to find a buyer?	2	10%	14	70%	4	20%

One local Indian arts dealer who does not sell prehistoric items
reports that individuals come to his store 3 or 4 times a week during
the summer and ask if he is interested in buying prehistoric artifacts.
Usually they have fewer than 5 pieces for sale, but occasionally they
have whole collections. He also reports that buyers are not difficult
to find, and that there are several local outlets which buy on the spot.
He observed that the antiquities market could be a very lucrative business, and that collectors from a widespread geographical area are
interested in buying through dealers. It is recognized by both this
dealer and by Group 3 collectors that illegality drives prices up and
the stiffer the fines, the higher the risks involved and the higher the

prices on the antiquities market. Collectors, artifact dealers and
any other middle men who purchase from diggers create a demand. If a
legal market could be enforced, prices would drop and the illegal trade
would fall off. This, however, requires some enforced record-keeping
of proveniences of a dealer's inventory which oversteps BLM's law enforcement authority (Douglas Scott, personal communication). A legal
market also implies destruction of archaeological sites on private
land, even if the destruction is legally sanctioned.

The role of the art market in encouraging looting of archaeological sites has been long recognized (Meyer 1973). The popularity of
Native American art in the early 1970s resulted in record prices for
prehistoric and historic items. Meyer (1973:11) quotes Stewart Peckham
of the Laboratory of Anthropology in Santa Fe:

> Although he (the pot hunter) deserves eternal damnation, he
> isn't the only one to blame. The affluent art collector
> should also be roasted in hell. His demand for new conversa-
> tion pieces to add to his collection, regardless of price,
> only stimulates the pothunter to seek out and pillage major
> archaeological sites.

Archaeology and Archaeologists

Most informants know archaeologists (Table 20). Many mentioned
names of professionals who live or work in the Montelores area as
personal friends or occasional visitors.

Table 20. Familiarity with archaeologists and archaeology.

question	# informants (n-20)				
	yes	%	no	%	no answer	%
Do you know any professional archaeologists?	17	85%	3	15%	0	0%
Have you talked to any lately?	7	35%	13	65%	0	0%
Do you think an archaeologist's work is different from what others do when they hunt or dig for objects?	17	85%	2	10%	1	5%

The difference between archaeologists and artifact hunters is
observed to be in motives (public knowledge vs. individual gain) and
methods (archaeologists are usually but not always more meticulous).

The most careful and well-constructed answer to how archaeologists and artifact hunters differ comes from a woman who has worked extensively with archaeologists:

> Archaeologists, I know, are not more careful; they are not more thorough. However, they have a knowledge of the whole field; they know more about what they're looking for other than artifacts. When we first started digging, we knew nothing. Now, after years of experience, we have learned a lot. Archaeologists know when they begin to dig.

This is a respectful and generous estimate of professional training.

Aside from some cynical answers to the question, "What do archaeologists do?" ("They waste time and money"), most stressed the digging and culture history aspects of fieldwork and a few mentioned preservation aspects. Some people are aware and concerned that poor archaeologists are allowed to work in the region and that people considered to be pothunters sometimes not only know more but are more careful in excavating sites than these members of the professional community.

> With some archaeologists, there is no difference between them and diggers. The good ones are hunting for history and the study of man. Individual differences in archaeologists mean a lot. _____ has destroyed in a year's time more than other diggers destroy in a lifetime. Also _____. He didn't know half as much as many diggers. He should never have been allowed in the field. He was digging with a backhoe. But _____ really did a good job.

It may be significant that so few tied archaeological research to environmental problems or present or future practical applications. A lack of public knowledge about goals of archaeological research and cultural resource management is apparent. An update on Ascher's 1960 article on the public image of archaeologists would be enlightening. Little change seems to be evident between his observations that the public believes "objects and techniques, not ideology, are most important to archaeologists," and the sample's current opinions about what archaeologists do. Also apt is Green and LeBlanc's (1979:121) observation that "the problem of site destruction is in large part a result of the public's being taught the wrong lesson; that artifacts are valuable in their own right."

95

People were asked about the Dolores Archaeological Project
because it is the most highly visible, largest archaeological undertaking the area has ever known. However, feelings about the dam
itself certainly influenced opinions about the archaeological project.
Most people felt that although the archaeological project was partially
justified, too much money was being spent on archaeology for too little
return. Many felt that the archaeological project was holding up the
construction of the dam. Surprisingly little impact on the local
community was noted. Dolores Project archaeologists are seen as a
veneer of "imports" who will move on as soon as the project is over,
college students or transient workers rather than professionals. One
man says, "The archaeologists caused a lot of talking, lots of new faces.
We would notice the difference if they left, but we never associate with
them. The Hollywood (bar) did a booming business."

Opinion is split over whether the local community has been
involved and informed enough about the project. Many felt that the
information was available but local people had not expressed an interest
in it. One woman says, "Local people don't know enough about the project
but it would be hard to make them understand more . . . It's difficult
to reach people who are not interested in archaeology unless they are
somehow directly involved, for example, if Reclamation is buying their
land." There is also some feeling that local archaeological expertise
is not being tapped, and that many locals know more than some of the
archaeologists working on the project, who are consequently insecure
and condescending.

Table 21 summarizes opinions about the Dolores Project, Dolores
Project archaeologists and archaeologists employed by Federal agencies.
When people compared Dolores Project archaeologists to other archaeologists, they seemed to have a well-defined conception of what archaeologists in general are like, a less well-defined concept of Mesa Verde
archaeologists, and a poorly defined concept of archaeologists from
other Federal agencies. Archaeologists working for the private sector
or universities were differentiated from government archaeologists, but
this response probably has to do with strong feelings of polarization

96

between government and private sectors, not with differences actually perceived between archaeologists so employed.

Table 21. Dolores Archaeological Project opinions.

question	# informants (n-20)							
	yes	%	no	%	partially	%	don't know	%
Do you feel that the archaeological portion of the Dolores Project is justified?	7	35%	7	35%	5	25%	1	5%
Do local people know enough about it?	12	60%	8	40%	0	0%	0	0%
Have local people been involved enough?	9	45%	9	45%	0	0%	2	10%
Has the large number of archaeologists associated with the Dolores Project changed the community in any way?	7	35%	13	65%	0	0%	0	0%
Have you ever seen or talked with Dolores Project archaeologists?	15	75%	5	25%	0	0%	0	0%
Have the Dolores Project archaeologists done anything for the community?	10	50%	8	40%	0	0%	2	10%
Are these archaeologists typical of archaeologists in general?	12	60%	3	15%	0	0%	5	25%
Are they similar to archaeologists at Mesa Verde?	10	50%	3	15%	0	0%	7	35%
Are they similar to archaeologists from other Federal agencies?	7	35%	1	5%	0	0%	12	60%
Is there a difference between government archaeologists and archaeologists who work for universities or private companies?	9	45%	8	40%	0	0%	4	20%

An archaeologist originally from the area expressed some local attitudes he has observed toward archaeologists: (to paraphrase), Most people can't believe that someone is paid to do archaeology, in other words, to do needless work gathering superfluous information. People believe that we know everything we need to know about area prehistory, but some archaeologists have earned a long standing respect from locals. The Dolores Project has, in fact, hired not only three local archaeologists but many people who started out by working in

Youth Corps Projects. People observe archaeologists excavating more intensively than local diggers, i.e., digging roomblocks and kivas. It is obvious that they are after something other than "goodies," but what this might be is uncertain, and people do not have a clear idea of how or why archaeologists excavate. Another archaeologist believes that the purpose of the project has been misrepresented as a treasure hunt, and that those responsible for local understanding have not succeeded in de-emphasizing artifacts as the goal of digging.

Removal of artifacts from southwestern Colorado

It is very important to almost everyone that objects stay in the local area, as is shown in Table 22. A couple who expressed only a slight interest in archaeology say, "It's important that objects stay in the area so our children can see them and identify them with the area." Opinion is split about whether archaeologists or artifact hunters are responsible for removing the most artifacts, and estimates vary widely about how much has been removed. One man says, "99% of the artifacts that were once here have left the state." Another says, "Locals have traded and sold locally but not out of the area. There's much left here and there's a lot that came in, too." This contrasts somewhat with the attitude Williams (1977:69) reports from southeastern Utah that "collecting and saving artifacts by local people is the only means of assuring that cultural materials will remain in the vicinity of their origin, and out of the hands of archaeologists who may cart them hundreds or thousands of miles away to their home institutions for curation."

Table 22. Removal of artifacts from the area.

question	yes	%	no	%	don't know	%
Is it important to you that objects from sites stay in the area?	19	95%	1	5%	0	0%
Do you feel that archaeologists have removed much from the area?	11	55%	7	35%	2	10%
Do you feel that local artifact hunters and collectors have removed much from the area by selling or otherwise moving of collections?	9	45%	9	45%	2	10%

 # informants (n-20)

Amateur archaeological organization

Interest in an amateur archaeological organization is also divided. Ten informants of 20 expressed an interest in such an organization. It seems unusual that the Montelores area, probably the richest archaeological area in the state, has never supported an amateur archaeological organization. Distance, lack of professional guidance, lack of professional or academic resources, and highly individual and diverse interest levels are all factors that have hindered formation of such a group. A woman says, "One man formed a group in Cortez, but it didn't develop. They thought they would be volunteer helpers, but the archaeologists were not interested. They would have had a better chance with professional help but I still doubt if it would have worked out." The area offers much potential for an amateur organization and interest can be gauged by local participation in the Anasazi archaeology lecture series of summer 1979, which was consistently high (Ed and Jo Berger, personal communication). The series was planned so that lectures moved from place to place around the area, making it more convenient for a large cross-section of area residents to attend. One man interviewed volunteered to work in a local, informal law enforcement organization to keep others from digging on public land.

Lack of professional guidance may be related to the ambivalence archaeologists sometimes feel about amateurs. The technician-level skills of much excavation and analysis can be learned as quickly by a non-degreed person, thus blurring the distinction between the "professional" and the "amateur." Some concern was expressed by archaeologists interviewed that the Dolores Archaeological Project Youth Corps programs had produced a new, skilled generation of pothunters, and that an amateur organization would merely hone the talents of those already inclined to dig illicitly. Still, it seems that, given the size of the area to be protected and the proportionate lack of funding, any public help that may be forthcoming certainly should be accepted. How to accomplish this is another story. Hester Davis (1972:271), who is very optimistic about the potential for using amateur organizations in research and preservation contexts, nonetheless feels that "turning (amateurs) into an army of trained allies is almost a full time job."

Origin of artifact hunters

People feel that locals have been more consistently responsible
for digging and artifact hunting (Table 23), but that tourists and new
residents account for a significant amount of recent artifact hunting
activity, and that there has been a long history of non-residents who
make special trips to the area to hunt or dig. One man says, "It used
to be all locals who hunted or dug for artifacts. Now, it's more
tourists than locals." Another says, "There used to be lots of tourists
hunting for artifacts, from Durango and from other parts of the state.
They'd put up camp, climb all over the ruins and dig for a week. This
has slowed down." Still another says, "There's a difference in the
way locals and tourists hunt for artifacts. Locals do the damage.
Tourists have no time or knowledge of the ruin locations--they also
have more respect." A woman says, "It's hard for tourists to know
where to go."

Table 23. Origin of artifact hunters

question	# informants (n-20)							
	locals	%	tourists	%	both	%	neither	%
Do you feel that most people who hunt for artifacts are primarily:	9	45%	3	15%	7	35%	1	5%

Attitude towards the government

Respondents answer emphatically that the government does have the
right to tell people not to dig on public lands (Table 24) and it, in
fact, is responsible for protection of those cultural resources.
However, any attempt by the government to control what transpires on
private land is not tolerated. A deep-rooted abhorrence of increasing
government encroachment on private land and on individual rights is
apparent. Also evident is a lack of concern with surface collecting.
"The government has the right to tell people not to dig, but collecting
sherds and arrowheads from the surface is O.K." One man says, "The
government must keep diggers off public lands because too many people

are not careful." A driller says, "It depends on the context. . . public lands belong to everybody. We feel that BLM lands are our lands." Along a similar vein: "I don't believe the government has the right to tell people not to dig or collect on public land because the land belongs to the people. But people should leave ruins alone--they shouldn't tear them down."

Table 24. The government and cultural resources.

question	# informants (n-20)					
	yes	%	no	%	don't know	%
Does the government have the right to tell you not to dig or collect on public lands?	18	90%	2	10%	0	0%
Do you think that different government agencies have the same attitude about artifact hunters?	11	55%	4	20%	5	25%
Do you know what the term "cultural resources" means?	8	40%	12	60%	0	0%

Williams (1977:99-109) describes differences among three government agencies, the Bureau of Land Management, the U.S. Forest Service, and the National Park Service, in their approach to cultural resource management. He recommends a policy of consistency in objectives, policies and practices (1977:132) as a means of controlling vandalism and argues that selective preservation of resources may result in the interpretation that it is acceptable to collect or dig at some sites but not at others.

People interviewed see government agencies as more or less consistent in their approach to artifact hunting, although differences in agencies were often mentioned. Some sympathize with government problems in site supervision: "The government is hampered by districts that are so big that they are difficult to patrol or supervise." The BLM's efforts over the past 10 years in protecting ruins and enforcing the Antiquities Act have been observed. One man says, "The approach is changing and improving. Neither the Forest Service nor BLM used to have any interest. It was very hard to get a conviction with the law. The law and the attitude of government agencies has been strengthened

101

in recent years." The Forest Service was often cited as being the least concerned with cultural resources.

Definitions of the term "cultural resources" were accurate but uncertain, and less than half the people interviewed could define the term. It seems obvious that the less bureaucratic jargon used the better when getting an anti-vandalism message across to the public.

Artifact hunting

Characteristics of artifact hunters

Digging and surface collecting apparently used to be a family recreational activity (still is, to some extent) spurred on by the passion for archaeology of some family members. When it is not a family activity, it is an individual's interest and hobby. Archaeological sites are a part of the landscape in southwestern Colorado, as visible and ever-present as the canyons and as taken-for-granted by the people who have lived with them for generations. To those of us who visit, the sites are a source of wonder, but it is no more logical to think that everyone in southwestern Colorado would be interested in archaeology than it would be to think that these same people would cherish geology because they could see Ute Mountain every day. One man says, "We've always been around ruins, in the fields and so on. I became interested on my own, as a recreation." Table 25 summarizes learning and interest patterns for artifact hunting.

As a family activity, artifact hunting appears to be steadily decreasing because: 1) agricultural land is now nearly all cleared and interest excited by finds in the fields has now diminished. One farmer says:

> Having ruins on my own land led to my interest. First I
> destroyed them in the process of clearing land. Then I
> learned about their history by reading books. Then I
> saved them and made a study of them . . . Most of the
> land has been cleared, probably not over 10% uncleared
> land is left. The 1950's was the big time for buying
> and clearing land.

2) Grown children of older generation diggers are not interested, perhaps because of weakening ties to the land, perhaps because of access to faster-paced, contemporary recreational activities. As one

man says, "When life was slower and there was no TV and less entertainment, artifact hunting was more of a pasttime, more recreational than now." Another says, "In the old days, neighbors would invite you to come and dig with them. It was a recreational activity along with schoolhouse dances, horseshoes, and card playing parties." 3) BLM has clearly been more active in enforcing the Antiquities law during recent years, thus restricting artifact hunting to private lands.

Half of the people say they became interested in artifact hunting on their own, although five report becoming involved through their parents and six report an interest cultivated by childhood friends. Thirteen regard artifact hunting as a personal hobby, and 16 started when they were over 20 years old. Most hunt or dig infrequently. More people report artifact hunting as an activity of their friends than as something their parents did, and 12 report that their children enjoy hunting for artifacts.

Table 25. Learning patterns for artifact hunting.

question	# informants (n-20)			
	yes	%	no	%
Is artifact hunting or digging for artifacts a family activity?	10	50%	10	50%
Is this a personal hobby?	13	65%	7	35%

If you hunt or dig for artifacts did you first become involved in these activites through: (n-30)

your parents as a child	your friends as a child	your own interest	others as an adult	no answer/ not applicable
5 16.5%	6 19.8%	15 49.5%	2 6.6%	2 6.6%

When did you first dig or hunt for artifacts? (n-30)	0-5 years ago	6-20 years ago	over 20 years ago
	2 6.6%	5 16.5%	23 75.9%

How often do you go? (n-20)

once a year	4-5 times a year	once a month	more than once a month	no answer/ not applicable
12 60%	1 5%	2 10%	2 10%	3 15%

When was the last time? (n-20)

n/a	this week	this month	past 6 months	past 12 months	over one year ago
1 5%	2 10%	3 15%	1 5%	3 15%	10 50%

103

Table 25, continued

question	yes	%	no	%	no answer	%
Have your parents, or older family members, hunted for artifacts?	8	40%	12	60%		0%
Do your friends do this?	13	65%	6	30%	1	5%
If you have children, do they do this?	12	60%	6	30%	2	10%

informants (n-20)

80% of the people report knowing a few others who dig, most over 30 years old and most male, as summarized in Table 26.

Table 26. Extent, sex, and age of others who dig.

question	none		a few		half		most		all	
Of the people you know, how many hunt or dig for artifacts?	2	10%	16	80%	0	0%	1	5%	1	5%

informants (n-20)

	male		female		both males and females involved		no answer	
Are these people mostly:	11	55%	0	0%	8	40%	1	5%

	14-21		22-29		over 30		varies	
What are their age ranges primarily?	0	0%	2	10%	17	85%	1	5%

Prior to doing the interviews, we believed that artifact hunting was a local tradition in southwestern Colorado. The large number of private collections and personal histories from the Wetherill expeditions on up to the present of outings to ruins seemed to substantiate this. Sixteen of thirty people interviewed said they also regarded hunting and collecting as a local tradition. But closer scrutiny seems to support a family tradition model rather than a dispersed local tradition, and individual interest develops into or from this family tradition. Family traditions in archaeology and other professions conform to this pattern: continual exposure can provoke an interest on the part of children or other family members, but all archæologists' children do not follow in their elders' footsteps. One man sums it up, ". . . Many are not interested at all. It's not widespread enough to be a tradition. Many farmers see the ruins as an aggravation." It also seems that self-motivation is at least as important as family influence in cultivating an interest in archaeology. When asked if they were typical, most of the nine who said they were not cited depth of interest and commitment as the way in which they stood apart. It appears that some people also learned from an older generation of artifact hunters that were not a part of their family.

Habits of artifact hunters

As Table 27 indicates, it seems that most people go artifact hunting or digging alone or with one or two others (or with family) on weekends, usually with no planning. Spring is the preferred season and more than any other time, Easter weekend is the traditional time to picnic at a ruin. A named site in the area is the "Easter Ruin" for this reason. A portion of the interviews were conducted at Easter. On Easter Sunday, East Rock Canyon, a branch of McElmo Canyon with a large number of highly visible cliff dwellings, was crowded with family picnickers. Spring offers early pleasant weather and an opportunity to be outdoors after a long winter. Many large families live in the Montelores area, and ruins, often located in spectacular areas, provide an attractive locus for a get-together. It is not surprising that these cliff dwellings are picked clean of artifacts. The spring ground is moist and digging is easy. Winter snows and wash-out have uncovered previously buried artifacts. Many area families have trucks and access to canyons like East Rock Canyon and Sand Canyon, impossible through much of the winter, is not difficult once the roads are dry. Many people were seen hiking far from the access road.

Table 27. Artifact hunting habits.

question	# informants (n-20) (percentages shown are of total # responses)

Do you hunt for artifacts:
  (more than 1 answer possible)

alone	with 1-2 others	with 3-4 others	with more than 4 others	varies	no answer
9 36%	9 36%	3 12%	1 4%	2 8%	1 4%

Table 27, continued

(percentages shown are of total # responses)

What is the average time you spend?
(more than 1 answer possible)

2 hours	½ day	1 day	2 or more days	n/a
10 37%	5 19%	9 33%	2 7%	1 4%

When do you do these activities most often?
(more than 1 answer possible)

weekdays	weekends	holidays
3 14%	14 67%	4 19%

What time of day?
(more than 1 answer possible)

morning	afternoon	evening	night	varies
9 31%	11 38%	1 3%	0 0%	8 28%

In what season do you most
frequently do these activities?
(more than 1 answer possible)

spring	summer	fall	winter	not seasonal
14 54%	7 27%	3 12%	0 0%	2 8%

Do occupational responsibilities
(such as farm work) make a
difference as to when you go?

yes	%	no	%
19	95%	1	5%

How far ahead of time do you plan your trips?
(more than 1 answer possible)

no planning	less than 1 day	1-2 days	3-7 days	more than 7 days
16 76%	2 10%	1 5%	0 0%	2 10%

It should be stressed that these artifact hunting and digging patterns apply to those who view it as a recreation. Habits of commercial diggers are likely to differ. Williams (1977:52, 53) found that cultural resource managers do not perceive a pattern for when vandalism occurs. As Peter Pilles, Coconino National Forest archaeologist (quoted in Williams 1977:52-53) observes, however, commercial diggers may work during the week while casual artifact hunters go out on weekends and holidays.

Concerning characteristics of artifact hunters and diggers Williams' (1977:55) data conforms with interview data in most respects. 48% of cultural resource managers believe that the over-30 age group is responsible, compared with 85% of interview informants; 31% of the managers named the 14-21 age group as responsible, compared with 0% of the interview informants; 19% of the managers named the 22-29 age group, compared to 10% of the interview informants. Interview data supports Williams' (1977:58) view that older age groups not acting through "youthful exuberance or spontaneity" constitute the ranks of artifact hunters and diggers.

Williams' (1977:59) findings on whether artifact hunters act alone or in groups seem inconclusive, but 2 managers write that small groups (2 to 3) or lone individuals seem to be the norm. This concurs with interview results, with 72% of the informants reporting going alone or with 1-2 others. Results for sex of artifact hunters and diggers are also comparable: 55% of interview responses indicate that these people are male, and 0% are female, with 40% indicating that both men and women are involved (5% no answer). Williams (1977:61) reports that 77.2% of managers believe men are involved, 1.8% believe women are involved, and 21% believe that both are responsible.

Site preference: access and knowledge of site locations

The question of which sites are preferred by artifact hunters is at the center of the problem of how to manage and protect all sites. The sample indicates that people often return to the same site again and again, and that it is accessible by two-wheel drive car or pickup, in an area that is a traditional place to look and that has artifacts on the ground surface or not deeply buried so that finds encourage further investigation. People range over an area at least 20 miles in diameter. One farmer says, "Time and distance are the most important factors in deciding where to go." Another farmer says, "Friends and family recommend places to go. We used to go to likely places--there had been no digging in the canyon sites. Now there's no such thing as a remote untouched site. People feel that small places have been dug out (exhausted)." A long-time area resident says, "Families go to easily accessible places, where they can drive in with the kids and have the conveniences of home. Families also often return to the same general areas for years." Local people who dig are apt to be quite familiar with the land and they know where the ruins are located. It is consequently a matter of deciding which site to go to rather than discovering a place to go. Our data concur with Williams' (1977:66) evaluation that most artifact hunters and diggers do not drive long distances to get to sites, and are local people familiar with site locations.

One tendency worth noting is the universally expressed attitude that all the sites have already been destroyed and there is little worth preserving now. One man says, "All the ruins have been dug up for 70 years." Another says, "One place is as good as another, they've all been so badly picked over."

As described in Table 28, it seems that families and individuals prefer general areas close to where they live, but driving long distances to dig or surface collect is not unheard of. Fourteen of 20 have sites on their own property.

Table 28. Driving and walking distance to sites.

question   # informants (n-20)

What is the usual distance you drive
  to get to a site?

0-5 miles	6-10 miles	11-20 miles	over 20 miles	n/a
5 25%	4 20%	4 20%	6 30%	1 5%

mean farthest distance ever driven to a site: 60.93 miles (5 "no answers")

What is the usual distance you walk
  to get to a site?

0-100 yds.	101 yds.-¼ mile	¼-½ mile	½-1 mile	over 1 mile	n/a
6 30%	8 40%	3 15%	0 0%	2 10%	1 5%

mean farthest distance ever walked to a site: 3.3 miles (2 "no answers")

Walking more than a few hundred yards to get to a site is apparently unusual. The norm was expressed by one man: "We usually park right where we dig."

Table 29 deals with types of roads and vehicles used in access to sites. Maintained dirt roads account for 25% of access. "It's usually a maintained county road within a mile of places we go." Agricultural roads and oil and gas drilling access roads account for another 48% of access, although the breakdown in road types is somewhat misleading. On-the-ground inspection of the area leads to the conclusion that "agricultural access" and "oil and gas drilling access" may describe growth of the road network, but do not describe road conditions. Some of the above are in better condition than county-maintained dirt roads and some are jeep trails. When these two categories are combined with the "4-wheel drive" road category, 65% of access is accounted for. Importance of roads, especially jeep roads, as a factor in site vandalism in southwestern Colorado has been noted by Curtis Martin for the Sand Canyon area, and by Douglas Scott (1977). Lightfoot and Francis (1978:89) have also observed a tendency for severely vandalized sites in BLM's Little Colorado Planning Unit in northeastern Arizona to be located close to jeep roads or trails. In fact, "in several instances, unimproved jeep trails appeared to have no other purpose than to provide access directly to archaeological sites in the more remote regions of the Little Colorado Planning Unit." One informant expresses an identical viewpoint: "If a site is located off a road, people will drive off roads to get to it." A local archaeologist further observes that roads all over the Pleasant View area lead only to sites. The extensive existing road network makes walking long distances unnecessary, and this road network is rapidly expanding as oil and gas exploration accelerates.

People expressed divergent opinions that commercial pothunters would choose easily accessible sites so they could make a hasty escape, or would choose remote sites so they would be less likely to be spotted by patrols. Distance was not considered to be an obstacle for either truly interested people or commercial diggers.

Two-wheel drive truck is the usual vehicle driven to sites. Four-wheel drive vehicles are used only slightly more frequently than two-wheel drive cars. Use of motorcycles is uncommon (15% report having used motorcycles). Williams (1977:72-74) also reports that access by two-wheel drive vehicle is prevalent, although means of access varies by agency from walking to two-wheel drive to four-wheel drive. BLM managers reported nearly equal access percentages by two-wheel drive as by four-wheel drive vehicle.

Table 29. Road and vehicle use patterns.

question   # informants (n-20)
(percentages shown are of total # responses)

What type of roads do you drive on
  most frequently to get to a site?
  (more than 1 answer possible) (n = 52 answers)

paved	maintained dirt	4-wheel drive	oil/gas drilling access	agricultural access	drive off roads
3 6%	13 25%	4 8%	8 15%	17 33%	7 14%

What vehicle do you usually use to
  get there?
  (more than 1 answer possible)

2-wheel drive car	2-wheel drive truck	4-wheel drive vehicle	n/a
4 19%	10 48%	5 24%	2 10%

Have you ever used motorcycles
  in these activities?

yes	%	no	%	n/a	%
3	15%	16	80%	1	5%

Site preference: chained lands

Table 30 summarizes factors in site preference. The BLM fared badly on criticisms having to do with chained land. Clearly, people prefer sites in agricultural areas over sites on chained land for a number of reasons. Agricultural land is private, therefore a legal place to dig. Vegetation and ground cover have often already been removed. Sites in chained areas have frequently been partially destroyed by chaining and even if they are in good condition, chained areas are viewed as unpleasant ugly places. Sites in chained areas are easy to pick out, especially because of the thick vegetation or isolated stand of trees left on the site when the surrounding area was chained. Other characteristics people mentioned include higher visibility of mounds when the surrounding timber is down, different soil color, and easier access. Following are some critical comments on chaining:

> Sites are more obvious in chained areas because BLM has chained around the sites and left the trees on them. They destroyed the little sites. Now they're hollering about protection after they've done the damage themselves.

> BLM created a terrible mess by chaining.

> BLM's chaining has done as much or more destruction to structures than vandals.

Table 30. Factors in site preference.

question	# informants (n-20)			
	(percentages shown are of total # responses)			
	yes	%	no	%
Have you ever gone to sites in or near chained areas?	12	60%	8	40%
Do you prefer these sites?	3	15%	17	85%
Have you ever gone to sites in or near agricultural areas?	17	85%	3	15%
Do you prefer these sites?	15	75%	5	25%
Are the sites you go to easy to see and identify?	17	85%	3	15%

What is the land status of the areas you usually go to?
(more than 1 answer possible)

private		public		my own land		don't know		n/a	
14	47%	7	23%	7	23%	1	3%	1	3%

Which kinds of places do you prefer?
(more than 1 answer possible)

	#	%
large number of artifacts on the ground but no structures	6	12%
large rubble mounds	13	26%
small rubble mounds	15	30%
stone structures and cliff dwellings	12	24%
historic sites	3	6%
no answer	1	2%

Site preference: land status

Many who once dug on public lands or would like to dig on public lands are aware of stiff fines for the offense and where they dig is determined by which landowners will grant permission to dig on their land. One man says, "How often I go digging depends on the weather and whether I can get permission to dig on private land. I can't afford the fine for digging on public land." Another says, "Where I go depends 99% on where I can get the landowner's permission to dig."

Site preference: visibility and site features

Much of the questionnaire was tailored towards structural site types commonly vandalized in southwestern Colorado, i.e., prehistoric stone or adobe-walled dwellings, rock shelters, and rubble mounds. Although many other site types are found in the area, including historic structures, open campsites, sherd and lithic scatters, and rock art, the area is known for its very high site density of prehistoric structures and mounds. Questions dealing with surface collecting do not necessarily limit themselves to structural site types, but questions having to do with site recognition, features, and digging are aimed at them. More than other parts of the questionnaire, these questions have resulted in data specific to southwestern Colorado, where indigenous vegetation growth patterns and site architecture and location combine to make some sites highly visible.

80% of responses indicate a preference for large or small rubble mounds or stone structures and cliff dwellings (Table 30). Fascination with prehistoric mounds and structures is evident. Cliff dwellings in alcoves are not only easily recognized but highly visible, often from miles away. People also recognize sites by presence of a rubble mound (or "rock pile") and by the tall sage that grows on surface pueblos, preferred as well for their large easy-to-dig trash areas. Size of site is an obvious factor in visibility, although Lightfoot (1978:107) found in northeastern Arizona that sites with the largest room counts are not necessarily the most severely impacted; other factors such as access seem to mitigate the importance of site size. People also mentioned looking for sites on ridges or other vantage points in south-facing areas.

112

Table 31 summarizes factors considered when choosing sites to dig.

Table 31. Factors in choosing sites to dig.*

question	# informants (n-20) (percentages shown are of total # responses)	
Is it better to go to a site that:		
has already been dug into	3	8%
has not already been dug into	12	33%
has eroded naturally	5	14%
is locally well-known	3	8%
has a large number of artifacts on the ground surface	11	31%
no answer	2	6%

*more than one answer possible

Williams (1977:48-51) explored several factors managers considered to cause cultural resources to be vulnerable to vandalism. These were, in order of importance: 1) public knowledge of the resource ("resource is well-known, and people seek it out") - 60% response by managers; 2) previous vandalism - 56%; 3) location in an area of concentrated visitor use - 45%; and 4) deterioration due to natural weathering - 44%. Two other factors were written in frequently by respondents: value to person or market value (8%), and remote locations (8%). Those interviewed in this study were asked to rate some of these same factors, along with surface artifact density, in importance in choosing a site to dig (Table 31).

In contrast to Williams' findings, informants feel that best clues to a productive site are a large number of artifacts on the ground (31%) and pristine condition (33%). However, few if any sites are felt to be in pristine condition. The factor of previous vandalism is felt to be unavoidable rather than a matter of choice. Erosion (14%) and local knowledge of the site (8%) seem to be less important in choosing a site to dig. Comments on this topic are worth noting at length:

> All sites have been dug in. Old diggers dug up at least 50%. They went to the middle of the trash and spread out from there.

It depends on how thoroughly they've previously been dug.
Many diggers cover exploratory holes back and you can't
tell the sites have been dug. But diggers can miss a lot.
It takes a lot of ambition to dig. Natural erosion makes
no difference.

I've never been to a site that has not been dug into.

It makes no difference if you are just arrowheading. There
never would be a large number of artifacts on the surface
because they're all gone.

None of the above makes any difference. We've never been
to a site that hasn't been dug into. There aren't any.

I never saw any that hadn't been dug. Usually people have
potholed around and dug right in the middle.

For picnicking, sites already dug into are O.K., if they're
not destroyed. For those really interested in pothunting,
clean sites are best. Sites with large numbers of surface
artifacts can't last--people pick them all up. Sites close
to roads and easy to get to and well-known will be destroyed,
not intentionally but through wear and tear. They're very
fragile.

It makes little difference if a site is locally well known
except that it will probably be more disturbed.

There's not much difference in whether or not sites have been
dug, since most people who used to dig put in a pothole here
and there and left a lot in between. We have dug in very few
sites with natural erosion. Artifacts, especially arrowheads,
often indicate subsurface material in beanfields.

There's no place that hasn't been dug into. Sites are recreational places to visit, pleasant places to picnic at.

People don't think about natural erosion, although it often
pinpoints the best places to look.

Sites are often popular places to go. Sherds on the surface
make them more interesting.

A past BLM ranger relates that Westwater Ruin, a vandalized ruin
in southeastern Utah, was excavated by the Utah State Archaeologist's
Office and many artifacts were found at the site, which consequently
received much press. This caused an upsurge in vandalism of sites that
had previously been badly vandalized. A local archaeologist believes

that the size of the trash mound is the deciding factor in which sites are chosen, rather than period of the site or accessibility. He has observed sites next to roads that have not been vandalized and vandalized sites away from roads. He has also observed that people do not return to the same site unless it is a big, productive site; some sites have been potted over a period of 50 years, with declining productivity. In his view, word of mouth and easy digging are also important factors. Known areas are preferred for surface collecting, regardless of site type. Another local archaeologist believes that families have a clannish attachment to some sites.

That some people prefer certain kinds of sites is also substantiated by familiarity with individual pothunting styles through extensive patrol. Government field personnel have been able to recognize footprints, tire tracks, and recent trash at sites, screening and digging styles, and preferences of some individuals for sites with eroding burials or sites located in certain kinds of topography (Fred Blackburn, personal communication). The infamous "granola bar" vandal, apprehended on U.S. Forest Service lands in southwestern Colorado, left a signature of granola bar wrappers at sites he potted.

As Table 32 illustrates, 60% of the informants say they can date sites, and they employ Pecos classification periods. Date indicators include pottery, site size, architecture, and the remainder of the artifact inventory. Pecos classification periods are known to describe characteristics of sites that determine whether or not they are easy to dig or productive--for example, size of trash mound. Sites are chosen on the basis of these latter features rather than on the basis of period, unless diggers are looking for specific artifacts they know to be associated with certain periods--for example, classic Pueblo III pottery. Vandalized sites may thus seem to cluster by period. The antiquities market may also determine which periods of sites are dug by value placed on certain kinds of artifacts. In Utah, Pueblo II sites are dug for their redware and Kayenta style pottery. In southwestern Colorado, Pueblo III sites are dug for their Mesa Verde Black-on-white mugs and bowls.

Table 32. Site dating and preference.

question	# informants (n-20)			
	yes	%	no	%
Can you tell how old a site is?	12	60%	8	40%
Do you prefer to go to sites of a certain age?	8	40%	12	60%

Intra-site preferences

As Table 33 indicates, 60% of responses state that the trash area is the best place to dig once a site is located, although previous vandalism to trash areas may account for new vandalism to other parts of sites. One man with extensive excavation experience says, "Forty years ago, the trash area was best. Now the sites have already been picked over. Today, it's just where you get lucky and find something." Another man says, "Family type digging was in trash mounds. A family goes for the easy parts. Vandalism to rooms is by people who sell. Locals don't want to work that hard." People have specific ideas about which side of the ruin the trash is on and where burials are located. Only those interested in other aspects of archaeology besides artifacts, or those interested enough in dealing to spend the time and effort to excavate roomblocks and depressions, are thought to dig in anything but trash. Diggers look for burials because pottery is found in burials, and they prefer sites with large trash mounds because they believe that this is where burials are found. Peter Pilles describes the same pattern in Arizona: "They (pot hunters) first concentrate on the trash burial areas until the burials are pretty much wiped out. Then their attentions are turned to the pueblo itself, unless the burials are initially found to be within the rooms, in which case the pueblo is wiped out."

Table 33. Digging habits.

question	# informants (n-20) (percentages shown are of total # of responses)											
Once you are at a site, where is the best place to collect or dig? (more than 1 answer possible)												
	trash area		rooms		depressions		other		don't know		none	
	15	60%	2	8%	1	4%	5	20%	1	4%	1	4%

116

question	# informants (n-20)
	(percentages shown are of total # of responses)

What tools do you use?
(more than 1 answer possible)

shovels	screens	trowels	rakes	power equipment	other	none	n/a
18 42%	8 19%	8 19%	1 2%	2 5%	4 9%	1 2%	1 2%

How much time do you spend digging?

0-2 hours	3-4 hours	5-8 hours	over 8 hours	n/a
7 35%	3 15%	4 20%	4 20%	2 10%

Is it best to dig:

a few large holes	several small holes	don't know	n/a
4 20%	10 50%	3 15%	3 15%

	yes	%	no	%
Have you ever found a burial?	15	75%	5	25%
Are you looking for burials?	9	45%	11	55%

Equipment and techniques

As Table 33 shows, shovels are the most commonly used digging tools, although many use screens, trowels, and burial probes. Some report using power equipment. Serious diggers are careful about breakage and use small tools like trowels to excavate delicate objects, along with waiting for a time when the ground is wet or damp so that careful excavation will be easier. A woman whose family has dug in the area for generations reports that they used "screens for beads, needles, and so on. Trowels so as not to break things. We used a rod to look for slabs covering burials."

People dig small, exploratory holes rather than large holes, although there are those who are much more thorough and excavate room blocks or dig by trenching. Most recognize sterile soil and may start at site perimeters and work inwards. Burials are viewed, among those with a serious intent, as the most rewarding part if not the sole purpose of digging. Among those who had found burials (15 of 20), six reported reburying the bones and 3 reported collecting bones. One man describes his excavation techniques: "I get a front going and move it back in a solid trench. You

no real interest in digging, but not those who do have a real interest and not surface collectors. Signs do not inform local people of ruin location, since most large ruins are locally well known, but they may inform new residents or tourists. One man says, "Signs discourage the honest man but not the professional pothunter." Another says, "Signs discourage picnickers but not pothunters." Although it is recognized that there is an element that will pothunt despite all preventative measures ("If people really want to dig or collect, they will"), closing roads is thought to be the most effective measure in keeping people away from ruins, but anger and irritation at the government for blocking access may also result. "Closing roads would definitely keep people away." Distance is the barrier. One man expressed the opposite opinion, "Professional diggers are out on foot. If the roads were closed, they wouldn't have to worry about patrols."

Table 36. Effectiveness of preventative measures.

	yes	%	no	%	# informants (n-20) no answer	%	maybe	%	don't know	%
Have you ever seen a sign post saying that collecting or digging on public lands was illegal?	17	85%	3	15%	0	0%	0	0%	0	0%
Did this discourage you?	10	50%	8	40%	2	10%	0	0%	0	0%
Did this make you aware of ruins you previously did not know about?	5	25%	14	70%	0	0%	1	5%	0	0%
Have you ever seen any BLM personnel out on patrol?	10	50%	10	50%	0	0%	0	0%	0	0%
Have you ever talked to any BLM personnel on patrol?	8	40%	11	55%	1	5%	0	0%	0	0%
Do you think that fences or other physical barriers keep artifact hunters away from ruins?	6	30%	13	65%	0	0%	0	0%	1	5%
Do you think that closing roads and trails keeps people away?	9	45%	10	50%	0	0%	0	0%	1	5%

It has been the BLM's experience in the Sacred Mountain Planning Unit that pothunters are very organized and have used CB radios to relay information ¿ ⅃ᴜ the whereabouts of patrols (Max Witkind, personal communication). Air patrol, especially helicopter patrol, is considered to be a much more effective measure than ground patrol. The Montezuma County Sheriff's Office, under contract with BLM during summer of 1979 for cultural resource patrol, agrees with this assessment. Major entry roads to BLM lands have been patrolled, but an even more effective measure, according to a local archaeologist, would be to hire or somehow enlist local farmers to report pothunting or suspected pothunting. In any case, BLM's patrols have not been highly visible in the area. Only 50% of the sample, most of whom live or work in areas patrolled, have ever seen BLM personnel out on patrol.

Williams (1977:83-87) cites managers' comments on effectiveness of a variety of preventative measures. Patrol was thought to be best for stone or adobe-walled dwellings, with posting of signs "moderately effective." Erection of physical barriers and closing off roads and trails were rated respectively as "quite successful" and as having the greatest impact for protection of these resources. Patrol is considered to be most effective when used in combination with other techniques, especially interpretation.

Table 37 lists response to questions dealing with awareness of Antiquities Act convictions. 65% of those interviewed had heard of convictions.

Of those who had heard of Antiquities Act convictions, 8 of the convictions were in the Four Corners states, 4 were in the local area, and 2 were elsewhere; 10 were in the past three years. One man says, "News of convictions would act as a deterrent if it were in the local papers." Another says, "News of convictions would not stop arrowhead hunting but it would stop people who are not yet established pothunters."

Table 37. Awareness of Antiquities Act convictions.

question	# informants (n-20)			
	yes	%	no	%
Have you ever heard of anyone being convicted, fined or jailed for artifact hunting on public lands?	13	65%	7	35%
Have you ever heard about anyone in south-western Colorado being convicted on this charge?	6	30%	14	70%
Do you feel that such news would act as a deterrent to artifact hunting?	15	75%	5	25%

Table 38 summarizes effectiveness of public information efforts on those interviewed. The New Mexico news has had an impact on southwestern Colorado television viewers, since most area television comes from Albuquerque. News of New Mexico convictions and public information programs denouncing vandalism to archaeological sites have been seen by local people. Few Colorado efforts along these lines have reached southwestern Colorado, but local public information efforts have had an impact. Informants recalled newspaper articles appearing in the Montezuma County Journal over the past 2 or 3 years, and most of those interviewed commented on an article explaining the new Antiquities Law that was printed in early April during the interview period. Whether or not archaeology and the preservation ethic are taught in school seems to depend ultimately on the motivation of individual teachers.

Cultural resource managers strongly supported interpretation and public education as an additional control measure believed to be potentially effective (Williams 1977:92-94). Williams (1977:94-95) refers to several studies which show that public involvement is important in reducing vandalism.

Table 38. Effectiveness of public information.

question	# informants (n-20)					
	yes	%	no	%	don't know	%
Have you ever heard any radio or television programs or announcements telling people not to hunt or dig for artifacts or stressing the importance of preserving "cultural resources?"	8	40%	12	60%	0	0%
Have you ever seen any local newspaper articles on this subject?	17	85%	3	15%	0	0%
Have you ever heard of anyone giving a talk locally on this subject?	14	70%	6	30%	0	0%
Is this message taught in school locally?	4	20%	7	35%	9	45%

The sample sees digging and collecting as decreasing rapidly in the area at present. One person says, "I don't know of anybody who pothunts. It's a problem, but only a small number of people are involved." Table 39 summarizes these opinions.

Table 39. How widespread is digging and collecting
in this part of the state?*

	# informants (n-20)	
	(percentages shown are of total # of responses)	
everyone does it	2	7%
most people do it	0	0%
about half the people do it	1	4%
a few people do it	4	32%
a small minority of people do it	16	57%

*more than 1 answer possible

The final questions on the questionnaire solicited opinions on
how cultural resources should be managed, how many sites should be protected, and how to go about protecting sites. A wide variety of
opinions were expressed. These are presented verbatim as Appendix F.
In all, the opinions are not hostile to archaeology, to archaeologists
or to the government; they voice a concern for protection and stabilization of cultural resources, as long as private land and individual
rights are preserved.

As Table 40 summarizes, slightly more than half of the people
interviewed (56.1%) feel that a few significant sites should be protected in some way. The wording of this question is somewhat ambiguous.
The phrase "protected in some way" covers a great deal of territory.
It may have been interpreted to indicate some form of active protection
such as fencing or patrol of every site, rather than the passive protection plan the BLM now adheres to, with avoidance of impact and patrol
of large areas as its major components. Several informant ideas on cultural resource management deserve comment. First is the frequently
expressed support of a Mesa Verde-style park for protecting significant
sites, with recreation, interpretation, and stabilization but not
necessarily excavation as important features. Second is the idea that
some areas should be made less accessible and energy-related roads
should be blocked after use. Third is the widely expressed viewpoint
that the manpower it would take to adequately protect ruins would create
a dangerous precedent for increased government presence in the area.
Linked with this is the idea mentioned by several people in the sample

that the government's next step in controlling pothunting is the confiscation of private collections. The origin of this thought is unknown, but it drew strong negative reactions from all those who repeated it.

Table 40. Preservation attitudes.

question	# informants (n-20)	%
Please check the attitude closest to your own:		
all these sites should be protected in some way	4	14.2%
most of these sites should be protected in some way	1	3.3%
a few significant sites should be protected in some way	17	56.1%
there are so many sites that the ones already protected are sufficient	8	26.4%

Summary

Twenty interviews were conducted in the Montelores area of southwestern Colorado, using as a guideline a seven-page questionnaire developed to record feelings and habits concerning archaeologists, archaeological sites, artifact hunting and digging, and cultural resource management. A non-random sample of people known to have an interest in archaeology, digging, or collecting was chosen for the interviews. Responses were either tallied and have been presented in tables, or recorded verbatim and are presented in the text and in Appendix F.

To briefly summarize topics covered during the interviews:

1. The sample consists of people who show three levels of interest: 1) casual surface collectors; 2) those with collections who are mostly interested in digging for the sake of artifacts; 3) those who have an interest akin to archaeologists', not specifically tied to artifacts.

2. Collections are felt to be important family heirlooms. Sale of collections would not increase interest in artifact hunting. No local museum is available for display of collections, and museums are distrusted for not displaying collections and for alleged poor care of objects.

3. Few people know of others who sell artifacts, especially on a regular basis, but buyers are thought to be easy to find. Sale of artifacts can be expected to increase during hard times.

4. Archaeologists are felt to differ from artifact hunters in motives (public knowledge vs. individual gain) and methods (archaeologists are usually more meticulous), but archaeological research was linked with procurement of artifacts and not with social or environmental problems or cultural resource management goals such as preservation.

5. Dolores Project archaeology is thought to be excessively expensive for the "return," and the "return" consists of publications not to be seen for years to come and artifacts. Dolores Project archaeologists have made only a slight impact on the community. People feel that an opportunity to learn about the project has been offered.

6. Those interviewed feel strongly that artifacts with local provenience should stay in the area. They blame archaeologists and artifact hunters equally for removal of artifacts.

7. Interest in an amateur organization is divided, but local attendance at a lecture series on Anasazi archaeology during summer 1979 was high.

8. Pothunting as a recreational activity on public lands seems to be gradually diminishing as a generation of collectors grows older. Tourists and new residents continue to hunt for artifacts, however, as do a group of interested under-30 locals who restrict themselves to private land. Commercial pothunters undoubtedly are still at work in southwestern Colorado, locals feel, but not on the same scale seen in southeastern Utah, New Mexico, or Arizona.

9. People feel strongly that the government is responsible for managing and protecting ruins on public lands, but any interference on private land is intolerable. Differences are perceived in attitude towards cultural resource management on the part of different agencies, but not to the extent that digging on public lands is ever considered legal or acceptable.

10. Digging and collecting used to be a family tradition in southwestern Colorado, but always was characterized by some individuals who developed a strong personal interest. For several reasons, recreational

artifact hunting appears to be decreasing in recent years, and people report knowing few others who dig and collect.

11. Most diggers are over 30 and male, and most go alone or with 1 or 2 others. Weekends and holidays are preferred times, and spring is the traditional season to dig. Little planning precedes trips.

12. Sites are chosen by familiarity with a local area and ease in access. Most do not walk over a few hundred yards to get to a site. High visibility and private land status were other factors in site preference.

13. Most people drive two-wheel drive trucks on maintained dirt, agricultural, and oil and gas drilling access roads to get to sites.

14. People are looking for burials for the artifacts they contain and prefer to dig in trash areas at sites. Few if any sites are felt to be in pristine condition, and people do not seek out undisturbed sites. Natural erosion also seems to make little difference in choice of a site to dig. Many date sites using the Pecos classification. The antiquities market may influence choice of sites to dig by establishing high monetary value for certain artifacts.

15. People interviewed know that digging and collecting on public lands is illegal, and they feel that everyone else in the area also knows. Further interpretation or knowledge of the Antiquities Act is vague, however. The law was not taken seriously until recent government enforcement and prosecution efforts.

16. Closing roads is considered to be the most effective preventative measure for controlling pothunting. BLM patrol does not appear to be highly visible. Signs promote public awareness of the law and discourage those who are not serious diggers.

17. Awareness of Antiquities Act convictions seems to be growing. Many people have seen or heard local news presentations with an anti-vandalism message.

18. Most feel that at least a few significant sites should be protected in some way, and they offer a variety of opinions and ideas for how this should be done.

As a final note to this section, we would reiterate the fact that only those informants who consented to be interviewed and to complete the questionnaire are included in the sample and subsequent analysis. As a result, it is likely that a segment of the artifact hunting population is not accurately represented in the results of the study. It is probably indicative that the more serious or commercial pothunter is in the minority, however, since, of the potential interviewees contacted, only three out of 23 refused to meet with the interviewer. The three refusals were emphatic denials and unquestionably related to a strong belief in not discussing their collecting activities. If we project these figures for the sample, keeping in mind that it is a limited one, it may be posited that about 13 percent of the collectors are involved in such activities to the point they feel their actions should not be made public.

It should also be stressed that this small sample is non-random and was chosen on the basis of specific interests and activities. It cannot be said to represent the views or the behavior of the people of Montezuma County or of southwestern Colorado at large.

VI

FACTORS AFFECTING VANDALISM
AND
RECOMMENDATIONS

General

In this final chapter we seek to summarize information relating to delineation of the primary factors leading to the vandalism of cultural resource sites in southwestern Colorado, and to present recommendations which we believe may be critical to future amelioration of the overall problem. It is clear from the foregoing data presentation that the issue of intentional destruction of archaeological resources is not at all a simple one. Many interwoven factors contribute to the situation, leading one to the realization that the solution(s) will not be easily achieved. Nonetheless, as discussed below, we believe that positive steps have been taken to preserve the resource base and yet, at the same time, other avenues exist which will help in solving the problem. We also note encouraging signs, especially during the interviews with collectors, that inroads are being made in popularizing the theme that vandalistic activities are, in all instances, harmful to the public resource in question. Seemingly, only the malicious vandals, who fortunately exist as a small minority, are unaware of or are unconcerned with the potential scientific, educational, and other values which may be attributed to cultural resources of all types.

Factors Affecting Vandalism

It is evident that the principal factors underlying the vandalism of archaeological sites in southwestern Colorado are those which have been previously identified in the literature (cf. Harden 1979; Rippeteau 1979; Scott 1977). These include the following: 1) the density, distribution, and visibility of archaeological resources in the project area; and 2) the relative ease by which access may be gained to sites where digging and/or surface collection may be undertaken.

Beyond these primary factors, others we have examined include:

1) historical aspects of the overall problem,

2) the association between other types of land disturbing activities (e.g. chaining and agriculture) and site vandalism,

3) other characteristics and patterns of local artifact diggers and collectors,

4) attitudes of diggers and collectors towards cultural resource protection and government agency policies,

5) the effects of increased protective activities on the part of government and the pursuit of legal action against offenders of antiquities laws, and

6) the prevalence of commercial exploitation and the extent of an antiquities market in southwestern Colorado.

Information pertaining to each of these issues has accrued from a variety of sources, including perusal of the pertinent literature, review of the known site file data, a field implementation phase, and informant interviews. One observation which can be made at this point is that there is a large degree of concordance between the site file/ field data and the information gained from the interviews regarding types and methods of pothunting, kinds of sites at which such activity takes place, and so forth. As a consequence, the extensive results discussed in Chapter V are considered to have significant credibility for use in the present analysis and for future management use.

History of the Vandalism Problem

We have seen that the collection of prehistoric relics in south- western Colorado has a history which coincides with the earliest settlement of the region. This is perhaps to be expected since the presence of archaeological sites can scarcely go unnoticed even by the most casual observer. While early explorations to the area were prin- cipally concerned with locating and recording economic minerals, they also served to call attention to the occurrence of numerous significant vestiges of the prehistoric Anasazi occupation of the Four Corners area. Given the omnipresent aspect of human curiosity concerning antiquities and a general lack of concern for anything but relics themselves, it is also not surprising that wholesale collecting and looting soon took place after settlement of the region.

In large measure, early collecting of antiquities was oriented toward a profit motive as private philanthropists, large museums, and even states not only sanctioned such activities but also took part in promoting the practice by purchasing collections of prehistoric implements and human remains. Economic slumps in the 1890s and even later in the Depression years of the 1930s brought about increased collection, primarily as a means to supplement income.

It appears that two cultural traditions have arisen in southwestern Colorado concerning collecting and digging for prehistoric artifacts. In the first case, the idea of amassing locally available relics has become a community tradition. It has occurred since settlement, and nearly everyone is aware of the potential for such activities. On the other hand, our informant interviews have revealed that individual family traditions are also prevalent. Relic collecting forms an important aspect of family activities and resultant collections are revered as family heirlooms which have sentimental rather than economic value. Often, family collections are tied to the lands farmed by a particular family over the generations, thereby adding to the personal importance associated with the collection. We might add, parenthetically, that our data indicate any collecting for commercial interests appears to exist quite apart from these family traditions.

As a consequence of all of this, the presence of the human values associated with pothunting and collecting is great. Such traditions are difficult to breach by public education programs which outline the deleterious effects of such activities on cultural resources. We note, in a hopeful vein, that our interviews reveal that the younger generation in the area does not appear to have the ardent interest in relic collecting that their parents and grandparents exhibited. It is probable that there is an awareness that the resource is finite in nature and that most of the sites have been pothunted to some extent. Also, as was observed by some interviewees, there are today many alternative forms of recreation which may be enjoyed with relatively more ease and gratification than digging in prehistoric ruins.

Access

Without a doubt, ease of access has a tremendous effect on site vandalism. Both the known data and the interviews indicate an overwhelming preference for prospective sites to be located within about a quarter-mile of a road capable of two-wheel drive access. Thus, the most desirable access road is a maintained dirt road or one associated with agricultural activities which is passable on an annual basis. Use of four-wheel drive vehicles and motorcycles is apparently not widespread at the present. Some informants, however, reported driving off roads to reach a site.

Type of Site and Form of Vandalism

There is a clear preference for the later (i.e. Pueblo II and III) sites for pothunting activities, especially ones with medium to large rubble mounds indicative of former roomblocks. It is at these former habitation sites that extensive midden or trash areas occur. Such features are well known as locales for discovering the highly desirable human burials and associated funerary artifacts. Additionally, the middens represent easier digging than the rock filled roomblocks. Kivas at open sites are apparently rarely considered as lucrative structures for pothunting due to the large amount of overburden and fill which must be removed to get to the floor. In the earliest decades of collecting, however, kivas in cliff dwellings were often cleared in the search for relics. In terms of raw figures, 60% of the informants indicated a preference for digging in the midden area of a site. Of the known potted sites, 67% of those with observable and documented digging exhibited destruction in the middens. Correspondingly, only 8% of the informants reported digging in roomblocks, but 35% of the known sites had potholes in the rubble mounds. Thus, middens are preferred on at least a ratio of two to one over roomblocks. Again, no kivas were reported as being excavated by the informants nor were any observed in the known site data.

Nearly every form of potential tool, from trowels to heavy machinery, is utilized. Predominant hand tools include, in addition to trowels, shovels, screens, and burial probes. Techniques employed also vary widely; however, a preference for many small exploratory holes was noted. Trenching was also documented as a common technique.

Association of Chaining and Agriculture and Site Vandalism

There is a strong association between agriculture and antiquities collecting. Much of this, of course, results from farming of private land holdings which contain prehistoric ruins. Many family collections originated through these activities. Further, as noted above, access roads for agricultural needs, which are mostly private as well, are heavily utilized by prospective collectors.

Chaining of pinyon-juniper acreages, on the other hand, apparently has a reverse effect as few informants stated a preference for collecting in such areas, and few potted sites have been recorded in these zones. Factors related to this situation seem to include chained lands being primarily public and, in all probability, a resultant "openness" in these areas. Public opinion regarding chaining was generally negative, however, as many believed the chaining process resulted in sanctioned destruction of many prehistoric sites.

Attitudes of Artifact Collectors Towards Cultural Resource Protection and Government Policies

Nearly all the interviewees are aware that collecting on public lands is illegal and most are knowledgeable about recent increased protective actions on the part of government agencies (e.g. signs, patrols, fencing, and public education practices). However, widespread ambivalent feelings were noted regarding the effectiveness of such protective measures as opinions were invariably split evenly on these questions. Interestingly, a majority felt the ruins on public lands deserved protection, but many believe protective efforts would be better if oriented toward only the more significant sites. Of consequence is· the observation on the part of most interviewees that laws concerning protection of antiquities have only recently been taken seriously, primarily a result of publicizing apprehension and trials of offenders.

Commercial Pothunting

The acquisition of antiquities for profit seemingly takes place on a minor scale as compared to personal and family collecting in southwestern Colorado. At the present, the practice probably is not as widespread as in other areas of the Southwest. We do not feel, however, that adequate data were gathered through our efforts to enable us to make quantitative statements about this form of vandalism. It does take place in the project area, but its extent is not known. Some local Indian arts stores and other enterprises commonly display artifacts for sale and a few other buyers are known to exist. A majority of the collectors we talked with were more interested in their collection as something personal and not for sale.

Recommendations

Before discussing what may be done in the future to reduce the amount of archaeological site vandalism in the project area, it is important to briefly examine what is currently being done to fight the problem. In this context, we are interested in extant programs and policies of the BLM Montrose District and the San Juan Resource Area, of which the Sacred Mountain Planning Unit forms a part.

The very existence of the contract calling for this report is indicative of the high value the Bureau places on the protection of the significant archaeological resource base found in southwestern Colorado. To this example, we may add the many contracts which have been awarded in the past for stabilization of sites (Fig. 22) so that particular resources are not allowed to deteriorate to the point of complete rubble. Of course, stabilization of certain ruins often coincides with interpretive and public education programs (e.g. Lowry, Escalante, and Dominguez Ruins) which together contribute to increasing public awareness with regard to the resource and prehistoric Anasazi lifeways. In other instances stabilization efforts have been conducted to check natural destruction of ruins, or to repair the effects of human vandalism.

In the past, several forms of active protective measures have been undertaken in the project areas. These include fencing of important

Figure 22. Two examples of protective stabilization of prehistoric ruin walls. Top - Escalante Ruin, Bottom - Lowry Ruin (BLM photo files).

sites (Fig. 23), air and ground patrols, posting of signs relating to
cultural resources (Figs. 24 and 25), and pressing for prosecution of
persons apprehended looting archaeological sites on federally managed
lands. Additionally, we may note the proposal by the Bureau to have
the area designated as a National Conservation Area, one facet of
which would involve increased protection for archaeological ruins.
Finally, BLM personnel have been active in issuing news releases on
topics concerning cultural resource protection and, whenever possible,
in giving public talks.

On the negative side, however, in spite of the obvious genuine
concern on the part of the BLM in pursuing the programs noted above,
the overall beneficial effects have been far below what they should be.
Simply put, levels of manpower commitment and budgets have been much
less than needed for effective site protection. An examination of the
patrols will suffice to substantiate this point. During the summers of
1978 and 1979, active surveillance of the Sacred Mountain Planning Unit
was undertaken by vehicle, horseback, hiking, and flying (on a limited
basis when funds permitted). The patrols were conducted by one temporary
employee, hired only for the summer months. This person, then, patrolled
by himself some 217,000 acres of remote BLM land. In 1980, even this
temporary position has been dropped as fulltime BLM personnel, further
saddled by budgetary cutbacks in even necessary travel, attempt to patrol
the area on an irregular basis as other duties allow.

In terms of suggesting avenues that should be incorporated into
BLM's cultural resource management plan for the Sacred Mountain Planning
Unit, our recommendations are that current policies, as listed
above, be continued, but expanded to the point where they become meaningful. It must also be understood that there can be no simple solution to
that which is obviously a complex problem.

First, the BLM should continue to demonstrate its intent to enforce
antiquities laws through: 1) patrol, especially helicopter patrol and in
cooperation with local sheriffs' offices; 2) pursuit of convictions for
offenders caught potting sites on public lands; and 3) continuation of
releases to newspapers and other local publicity mediums such as radio
and television and talks to the public. It is clear from our interviews

Figure 23.   Protective fencing of sites.   Upper - McLean Basin
Towers; Lower - Painted Hand rock art site (BLM
photo files).

Figure 24. Type of warning signs currently being placed along
access roads throughout the Sacred Mountain Planning Unit.

Figure 25. This photo illustrates the effective combination of
protective fencing and an interpretive/warning sign
at the McLean Basin Tower site.

that these measures have made a difference in local attitudes and
behavior in the past few years, and public awareness of the Bureau's
intent to protect cultural resources is widespread today.

Patrol can be handled in a number of different ways, many of
which directly depend on amount of available funding for site protection.
Helicopter patrol, as opposed to airplane, horse, or truck patrol, is
thought by Montezuma Sheriff's Office deputies and by BLM rangers and
archaeologists alike to be the most effective form of patrol. Many
informants had noticed helicopter patrol.

An agreement between BLM and the Montezuma County Sheriff's
Department in summer of 1979 outlined a series of vehicular patrol
routes to be followed by Sheriff's Department personnel on a weekly
schedule throughout the Montelores area of the Sacred Mountain Planning
Unit. This kind of agreement has several advantages: 1) it is in
keeping with BLM's role as a management rather than a law enforcement
agency; 2) it enhances BLM's public image in the area by using local
personnel familiar with local attitudes and problems; 3) it taps local
knowledge of past law enforcement problems, of families or individuals
with a history of digging, and of possibilities for commercial involvement; and 4) with proper orientation, it avoids a heavy-handed approach
to law enforcement which has characterized some Federal efforts, and thus
avoids alienating the local population, a potential source of help.

In employing Sheriff's Department patrol, the San Juan Resource
Area Office must provide a thorough orientation program, as well as
guidance during patrol seasons. They must require reports and they must
actively check on Sheriff's Department activities and progress.
According to interview data, concentrating patrol efforts on weekends and
holidays and on spring rather than summer or fall would have the largest
impact on recreational pothunting.

A second part of BLM's management program should consist of a
combination of other preventative measures: posting of additional signs,
erection of barriers, and especially evaluation of the access road system
throughout the area. Signs and fencing seem to have an effect on certain
segments of the public and should be considered as a relatively low cost

and long term means of site protection. Such features will not deter all vandals, but they can help to reduce such activities by increasing awareness that archaeological resources are protected by law on public lands.

The topic of controlling access throughout the planning unit is not a new one (Harden 1979; Scott 1977). Very simply, the construction of access roads in the area may result in an increased flow of people to the locale and consequently an increased accessibility to sites. Given the density of archaeological sites in southwestern Colorado, it is virtually impossible to construct a road of any length and not con-comitantly increase access to some sites. It remains to be seen, however, if subsequent closure of roads would be a major panacea. Fifty percent of the interviewees felt that closing roads and trails would not keep people away from ruins. Most were of the opinion that serious pothunters and collectors would not be deterred. Given the current popularity of off-road vehicles, it may be that an increase in the use of such modes for access to sites can be anticipated. On the other hand, air patrols could be utilized to mitigate vandalism of remote areas. The topic of road closure and tight control of new road construction is one which we feel must be addressed in-house by the BLM, carefully weighing all aspects such as recreation, natural resource exploitation, and the cultural resource protection problem.

The third focus of the program involves public education. Dissem-ination of information related to antiquities laws is critical to this approach. People interviewed, including those who deal in artifacts, know that hunting, digging, and selling artifacts from public lands is illegal, but they are uninformed about the laws in relationship to private land, the laws in relationship to surface collecting, or the laws in relationship to selling and dealing. Ignorance of the law is a convenient excuse for local artifact dealers, who claim to have never seen the law and who blame the government for laxness in their responsi-bility to inform the public. All retail outlets for Indian artifacts, historic or prehistoric, should be informed of the new law: the 1979 Archaeological Resources Protection Act should be briefly explained and dealers should be fully informed of what is legal and what is illegal, along with penalties. BLM should foster a relationship with local dealers that is watchful but not hostile. At present, there seems to be little more that can be done locally to control the private antiquities market.

Another part of the public education program concerns increasing the awareness of the populace about the value of preserving sites while at the same time exploiting local collectors and amateur archaeologists as a valuable resource. Along these lines, Hester Davis (1972) has presented a realistic assessment of the difficulties in launching a public education program in terms of commitment of time and personnel. Despite this, archaeologists need to share information with the public if the public is to be aware of its stake in the past. Archaeologists must lead training and orientation programs for government staff; they must give local talks and presentations, and they must work with school systems. Key people in public information must be impressed with the importance of site preservation. The sense of possessiveness that local people have about Indian ruins in southwestern Colorado must be used to advantage in communicating a preservation ethic. When research problems are discussed, plain language must be used to explain how social and environmental problems are relevant to current problems and how digging can ruin a site even when no artifacts are removed. Efforts also need to be made to alleviate the deep-seated prejudice against Indians that assuages any feelings of guilt about grave-robbing.

In conclusion, we feel that in recent years great strides have been taken toward ameliorating the vandalism problem. In the realistic sense, we must be aware that certain elements of society will continue to vandalize sites out of malice and for profit. As government agencies take a more active role in protecting what remains of the cultural resources on public lands, the collector's attention will turn to sites on private lands. However, sites on private lands are just as finite as those on federally managed holdings. Consequently, there can be no let-up in the effort to protect cultural resources. Indeed, if management and protection programs are to succeed, it will take an increased effort

142

on the part of land managing agencies, especially in the form of manpower and budgetary commitments. As a final note, we mention that perhaps the most optimistic part of our study was the apparent support for cultural resource management and protection of archaeological sites on public lands expressed by the local people interviewed as part of the project. It remains for land managers and the professional community to develop the interest and cooperation of local people as a living cultural resource.

REFERENCES CITED

Adams, Robert McC.
1971   Illicit International Traffic in Antiquities. American
        Antiquity 36:ii-iii.

Afton, Jean
1971   Cultural Analysis of Burial Goods from Certain Anasazi
        Sites. Southwestern Lore 37:15-26.

Anderson, Bruce A.
1978   The Antiquities Act of 1906, and Problems with the Act.
        Paper presented at the 43rd Annual Meeting of the Society
        for American Archaeology. Tucson.

Anonymous
1977   Cultural Resources: One Criteria for Land Use Planning.
        Our Public Lands 27(2):3-5.

Ascher, Robert
1960   Archaeology and the Public Image. American Antiquity
        25(3):402-403.

Bandelier, Adolf F.
1881   A Visit to the Aboriginal Ruins in the Valley of the Rio
        Pecos. Papers of the Archaeological Institute of America,
        American Series 1:35-135.

Beals, Ralph L.
1971   Traffic in Antiquities. American Antiquity 36:374-375.

Binford, Lewis R., et al.
1970   Archaeology at Hatchery West. Society for American
        Archaeology Memoir No. 24.

Brown, Ruth Southworth
1977   Searching for Links with the Past. The Denver Post Empire
        Magazine, May 22.

Chandler, Susan M., Alan D. Reed, and Paul R. Nickens
1980   Ecological Variability and Archaeological Site Location in
        Southwestern Colorado: The Class II Cultural Resource
        Inventory of the Bureau of Land Management's Sacred Mountain
        Planning Unit. Ms. report prepared for the Bureau of Land
        Management, Montrose District, and Centuries Research, Inc.
        Nickens and Associates, Montrose.

Chapin, Frederick H.
1892   The Land of the Cliff Dwellers. W. B. Clarke and Company,
        Boston.

Chokhani, Peruiz
1979   Destruction on the Public Lands: A Closer Look at Vandalism.
        Our Public Lands 29:9-11.

Clewlow, C. William, Patrick S. Hallinan, and Richard D. Ambro
1971   A Crisis in Archaeology. American Antiquity 36:472-473.

Collins, Robert B.
1978   A Proposal to Modernize the American Antiquities Act.
        Science 202:1055-1059.

Crampton, C. Gregory
1964   Standing Up Country: The Canyon Lands of Utah and Arizona.
        Alfred A. Knopf, New York.

Crofutt, George A.
1885   Crofutt's Grip-sack Guide of Colorado. Overland Publishing
        Co., Omaha.

Davis, Hester
1972   The Crisis in American Archaeology. Science 175:267-272.

DeBloois, Evan I., Dee F. Green, and Henry G. Wylie
1975   A Test of the Impact of Pinyon-juniper Chaining on Archaeo-
        logical Sites. In The Pinyon-juniper Ecosystem: A Symposium,
        pp. 153-161. Utah State University, College of Natural
        Resources, Utah Agricultural Experiment Station, Logan.

Fewkes, Jesse Walter
1896   Two Ruins Recently Discovered in the Red Rock Country,
        Arizona. American Anthropologist 9:269-270.

Fletcher, Maurine S., editor
1977   The Wetherills of the Mesa Verde: Autobiography of Benjamin
        Alfred Wetherill. Associated University Presses, Cranbury,
        New Jersey.

Francis, Julie E.
1978   The Effect of Casual Surface Collection on Variation in
        Chipped Stone Artifacts. In An Analytical Approach to
        Cultural Resource Management: The Little Colorado Planning
        Unit, edited by Fred Plog, pp. 114-132. Arizona State
        University Anthropological Papers No. 13. Tempe.

Gaede, Marc, and Marnie Gaede
1977   100 Years of Erosion at Poncho House. The Kiva 43:37-48.

Garrison, E. G.
1975   A Qualitative Model for Inundation Studies in Archeological
        Research and Resource Conservation: An Example from Arkansas.
        Plains Anthropologist 20:279-296.

1977 Modeling Inundation Effects for Planning and Prediction. In Conservation Archaeology: A Guide for Cultural Resource Management Studies, edited by M. B. Schiffer and G. J. Gumerman, pp. 151-156. Academic Press, New York.

Graybill, Donald
1974 Measurement of the Amount and Rate of Site Destruction in Southwestern New Mexico. Paper presented at the 39th Annual Meeting of the Society for American Archaeology. Washington, D.C.

Grayson, Donald K.
1976 The Antiquities Act in the Ninth Circuit Court: A Review of Recent Attempts to Prosecute Antiquities Act Violations in Oregon. Tebiwa 18(2):59-64.

Green, Dee F.
1974 Lithic Sites of the La Sal Mountains, Southeastern Utah. Forest Service, Intermountain Region, Archeological Report No. 3. Ogden.

Green, Dee F., and Steven LeBlanc, compilers
1979 Vandalism of Cultural Resources: The Growing Threat to our Nation's Heritage. USDA Forest Service, Southwestern Region, Cultural Resources Report No. 28. Albuquerque.

Harden, Fred
1979 Cultural Resource Surveillance Report: Summer 1979. Ms. report on file at Bureau of Land Management, San Juan Resource Area, Durango.

Harris, Marvin
1968 The Rise of Anthropological Theory. Thomas W. Crowell Co., New York.

Hayes, Alden C., and Clifford C. Chappell
1962 A Copper Bell from Southwest Colorado. Plateau 35:53-56.

Holmes, W. H.
1878 Report on the Ancient Ruins of Southwestern Colorado, Examined During the Summers of 1875 and 1876. In Survey of the Territories for 1876, edited by F. V. Hayden, pp. 383-408. U.S. Geological and Geographic Survey of the Territories, 10th Annual Report. Washington.

1886 Pottery of the Ancient Pueblos. Bureau of American Ethnology, Fourth Annual Report, 1882-1883, pp. 258-360. Washington.

Hothem, Lar
1978 Indian Artifacting. Fur-Fish-Game August:26-40.

Hough, Walter
1901 Notes and News. American Anthropologist n.s. 3:590.

Ingersoll, Ernest
1885   The Crest of the Continent: A Summer's Ramble in the Rocky
        Mountains and Beyond. R. R. Donnelley and Sons, Chicago.

Ise, John
1961   Our National Park Policy. A Critical History. John Hopkins
        Press, Baltimore.

Johnson, Donald Lee, and Kenneth L. Hansen
1974   The Effects of Frost-heaving on objects in soils. Plains
        Anthropologist 19:81-98.

Johnson, Donald Lee, Daniel R. Muhs, and Michael L. Barnhardt
1977   The Effects of Frost-heaving on objects in soils, II:
        Laboratory Experiments. Plains Anthropologist 22:133-147.

Kessell, John L.
1979   Kiva, Cross, and Crown: The Pecos Indians and New Mexico,
        1540-1840. U.S. Department of the Interior, National Park
        Service. Washington.

Kim, Jae-On, and Frank J. Kohout
1975   SPSS: Statistical Package for the Society Sciences. 2nd ed.
        Norman H. Nie, et al., editors. McGraw-Hill, New York.

Lee, Ronald F.
1970   The Antiquities Act of 1906. National Park Service, Office
        of History and Historic Architecture, Eastern Service Center.
        Washington.

Lenihan, Daniel J., et al.
1977   The Preliminary Report of the National Reservoir Inundation
        Study. National Park Service, Southwest Cultural Resources
        Center, Santa Fe.

Lightfoot, Kent G.
1978   The Impact of Casual Collecting on Archaeological Interpreta-
        tion Through Regional Surface Surveys. In An Analytical
        Approach to Cultural Resource Management: The Little Colorado
        Planning Unit, edited by Fred Plog, pp. 91-113. Arizona State
        University Anthropological Research Papers No. 13. Tempe.

Lightfoot, Kent G., and Julie E. Francis
1978   The Effect of Casual Surface Collection on Behavioral Inter-
        pretations of Archaeological Data. In An Analytical Approach
        to Cultural Resource Management: The Little Colorado Planning
        Unit, edited by Fred Plog, pp. 82-90. Arizona State University
        Anthropological Research Papers No. 13. Tempe.

Lipe, William D.
  1977   A Conservation Model for American Archaeology. <u>In</u>
           Conservation Archaeology: A Guide for Cultural Resource
           Management Studies, edited by M. B. Schiffer and G. J.
           Gumerman, pp. 19-42. Academic Press, New York.

Lister, Florence C., and Robert H. Lister
  1968   Earl Morris and Southwestern Archaeology. University of
           New Mexico Press, Albuquerque.

Martin, Curtis W.
  1976   Archaeological Inventory of the Sand Canyon Cliff Dwelling
           Area, Montezuma County, Colorado. Ms. report submitted to
           the Bureau of Land Management, Montrose District Office.
           University of Colorado, Mesa Verde Archaeological Research
           Center. Boulder.

McNitt, Frank
  1957   Richard Wetherill: Anasazi. University of New Mexico Press,
           Albuquerque.

Meyer, Karl E.
  1973   The Plundered Past. Atheneum Press, New York.

Nickens, Paul R.
  1977   Colorado's Archaeological Sites Need Protection. Colorado
           Outdoors 26(4):7-10.

  1980   Archaeological Resources of Southwestern Colorado: An
           Overview of the Bureau of Land Management's San Juan Resource
           Area. Report prepared for the Bureau of Land Management,
           Montrose District.

Nordenskiold, Gustaf
  1893   The Cliff Dwellers of the Mesa Verde. P. A. Norstedt and
           Soner, Stockholm.

Noxon, John, and Deborah Marcus
  1980   The Moab Panel Site of Southeastern Utah: Its Defacement
           and Significance in Southwestern Prehistory. American Rock
           Writing Research Newsletter Vol. 1:5.80, pp. 1-3.

O'Rourke, Paul M.
  1980   Frontier in Transition: A History of Southwestern Colorado.
           Bureau of Land Management - Colorado, Cultural Resource
           Series No. 10. Denver.

Prudden, T. Mitchell
  1896   A Summer Among the Cliff Dwellers. Harper's Magazine,
           September, pp. 545-561.

1903   The Prehistoric Ruins of the San Juan Watershed in Utah,
        Arizona, Colorado, and New Mexico. American Anthropologist
        5:224-288.

1907   On the Great American Plateau. G. P. Putnam's Sons, New York.

Reyman, Jonathan E.
  1979   Vandalism and Site Destruction at Some National Parks and
          Monuments: A Call for Action. ASCA Newsletter 6:4-9.

Rippeteau, Bruce E.
  1979   Antiquities Enforcement in Colorado. Journal of Field
          Archaeology 6:85-103.

Robertson, Merle Greene
  1972   Monument Thievery in Mesoamerica. American Antiquity 37:
          147-155.

Roney, John
  1977   Livestock and Lithics: The Effects of Trampling. Ms. on
          file at the Bureau of Land Management, Winnemucca, Nevada.

Roper, Donna C.
  1976   Lateral Displacement of Artifacts Due to Plowing. American
          Antiquity 41:372-375.

Schiffer, Michael B.
  1976   Behavioral Archeology. Academic Press, New York.

Schroedl, Alan R.
  1976   Prehistoric Cultural Resources of Lake and Moqui Canyons,
          Glen Canyon National Recreation Area. Ms. report submitted
          to National Park Service, Midwest Archaeological Center.
          Department of Anthropology, University of Utah. Salt Lake
          City.

Scott, Douglas D.
  1977   Two Vandalized Pueblo III Burials: Some Key Factors Affecting
          Vandalism of Sites. Southwestern Lore 43(3):10-14.

  1980   Pothunting in Southwestern Colorado. Colorado Council of
          Professional Archaeologists Newsletter 2(1):3.

Scovill, D. H., G. H. Gordon, and K. M. Anderson
  1972   Guidelines for the Preparation of Statements on Archeological
          Resources. Ms. Arizona Archeological Center, National Park
          Service, Tucson.

  1977   Guidelines for the Preparation of Statements of Environmental
          Impact on Archaeological Resources. In Conservation Archaeology:
          A Guide for Cultural Resource Studies, edited by M. B. Schiffer
          and G. J. Gumerman, pp. 43-62. Academic Press, New York.

Sheets, Payson D.
  1973   The Pillage of Prehistory. American Antiquity 38:317-320.

Vivian, R. Gwinn
  1973   Archaeological Resources and Land-use Planning: An
          Archaeologist Speaks. Arizona Bureau of Mines, Fieldnotes
          3:1-7.

Williams, Lance R.
  1977   Vandalism to Cultural Resources of the Rocky Mountain West.
          Unpublished M.A. thesis. Recreation Resources Department,
          Colorado State University, Fort Collins.

Wood, W. Raymond, and Donald Lee Johnson
  1978   A Survey of Disturbance Processes in Archaeological Site
          Formation. In Advances in Archaeological Method and Theory,
          edited by M. B. Schiffer, Vol. 1, pp. 315-381. Academic
          Press, New York.

APPENDIX A

Completed preliminary version of vandalism record form
for archaeological site 5MT2137.

VANDALISM RECORD

See original form for sketch of
vandalism locations

Photo: Roll 1, Exp. 3, 4

1. Site No. |0|5|M|T|2|1|3|7|
2. Recorded By G & K Tucker
3. Institution Nickens & Associates
4. Date June 17, 1980

PREVIOUS RECORD (not necessary for previously unrecorded sites)

5. Name of Previous Recorder: D. Hayhurst   6. Date: 6-29-70
7. Institution: University of Colorado   8. Project: _____
9. Vandalism Noted: |2| 10. Description: _____
   1=Yes   _____
   2=No   _____
                                 _____
11. Photo of Vandalism: |2| 1=Yes   2=No

SITE CHARACTERISTICS

12. Site Type: 1=Yes 2=No   Architectural |1| Lithic |1| Pottery |1|
    Rockshelter |2| Hearth |2| Cist |2| Rock Art |2| Historic |2|
13. Temporal Period: 1=Yes 2=No   Paleo-Indian |2| Desert Archaic |2|
    Basketmaker II-(III) |1| Pueblo I |1| Pueblo II |2| Pueblo III |2|
14. Site Size: |3|7|5|0| | sq. m.   Ute or Navajo |2|

NATURE OF VANDALISM

15. Location of Disturbance: 1=Yes 2=No   Room Block |1| Midden |1|
    Pit Structure |2| Cist |2| Burial |2| Rockshelter |2| Rock Wall |2|
16. Method of Disturbance: 1=Yes 2=No   Shovel |1| Screen |2|
    Posthole Digger |2| Chain |2| Backhoe |2| Blade |2| Bullets |2| Graffiti |2|
17. Intensity of Disturbance: |1| | | % of Total Site Extent
18. Other Evidence of Disturbance: 1=Yes 2=No
    Footprints: Vibram |2| Regular |1| Cowboy boot |2| Other |1| Cattle
    ~~Estimated No. of Individuals~~ | |
    Fire: |2| Cigarette Butts: |2| Brand: _____
        Beverage Cans and/or Pull Tops: |2| Brand: _____
        Other Garbage: |1| one tin can
    Tire Tracks: Regular |2| Heavy duty (mud, snow) |2| Motorcycle |2|
        Other |2| _____
    Mounds of Artifacts: |1|

SPATIAL CHARACTERISTICS

19. Nearest Road and Rank   Distance: |3|0|0| | meters
    Rank |2| (1=principal access; 2=all weather; 3=seasonal use; 4=jeep road; 5=trail)
20. Nearest Community and Population Size   Distance: | |7|.|4| kilometers
    Size |3| (1=<100; 2=101-500; 3=501-1000; 4=1001-5000; 5=>5000)
21. Nearest Intrusion and Type   Distance: |0| | | |
    Type |6| (1=field; 2=well; 3=reservoir; 4=residence; 5=power line; 6=other line)   fence

---

22. Necessity of Site Surveillance: |1| 1=Yes   2=No
23. Comments: (use back)

154

ARCHAEOLOGICAL SURVEY SHEET

DEPARTMENT OF ANTHROPOLOGY   UNIVERSITY OF COLORADO

1. SITE NO. 5MT2137   2. COUNTY Montezuma   3. STATE Colorado   4. PHOTO NO. 3-3; MV 70-

MAP REFERENCE Mancos Quadrangle, U.S.G.S. 7½ Minute Series

6. TYPE OF SITE Surface Pueblo

7. CULTURAL AFFILIATION (IF KNOWN) BM III - P I

8. LOCATION Site is located atop a ridge running NW from North end of Weber Mountain, approximately 30' East of N - S fence dividing BLM and private land, approximately 300 yds. S - SW of 5MT2136.

SW ¼, NW ¼   SEC. 7   T. 35N   R. 13W

9. OWNER AND ADDRESS B.L.M.

10. PREVIOUS OWNERS

11. TENANT

12. INFORMANTS

13. PREVIOUS DESIGNATIONS FOR SITE

14. SITE DESCRIPTION POSITION AND SURROUNDING TERRAIN Elevation: 6890'. Drainage: Mancos River. Soil: Rocky, light brown. Vegetation: Pinyon, juniper, gramma grass. Site consists of standing slabs outlining 1) dwelling, and 2) possible cist; sheet trash is on N - S slope.

15. AREA OF OCCUPATION

16. DEPTH AND CHARACTER OF FILL

17. PRESENT CONDITION eroded

18. MATERIAL COLLECTED Sherds, chipped stone, axe

19. MATERIAL OBSERVED Sherds, chipped stone, axe, standing slabs; trash area has scattered rock rubble, mano fragments.

20. MATERIAL REPORTED AND OWNER

RECOMMENDATIONS FOR FURTHER WORK None

WAS SITE MAPPED BY SURVEY PARTY? Yes   WHAT TYPE OF MAP? Sketch Map

RECORDED BY D. Hayhurst   DATE 6/29/70

ARCHAEOLOGICAL FIELD RESEARCH

DEPARTMENT OF ANTHROPOLOGY

FORM   SITE 5MT2137   **UNIVERSITY OF COLORADO**   DATE 6/29/70

(Revised 6/17/80)

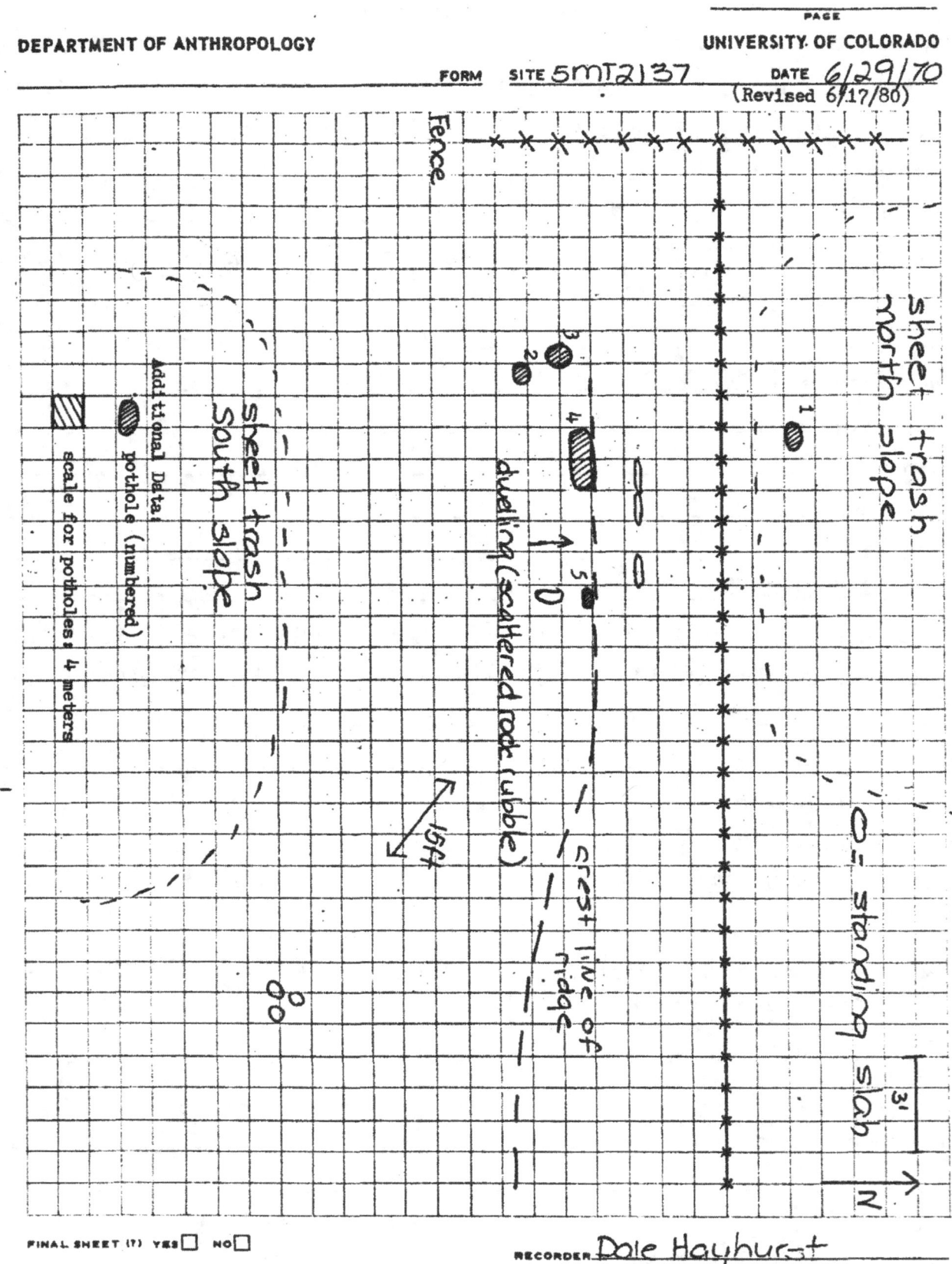

Fence

sheet trash
north slope

dwelling (scattered rock rubble)

sheet trash
south slope

Additional Detail
pothole (numbered)

scale for potholes: 4 meters

crest line of
ridge

15ft

O= standing slab

3'

N

FINAL SHEET (?) YES ☐   NO ☐

RECORDER Dale Hayhurst

APPENDIX B

Recommended vandalism supplement form

VANDALISM SUPPLEMENT

(A form for recording the nature and extent of intentional disturbance of a site
by human agents. This form should be completed in whole or in part whether the
site is vandalized or not, and attached to a completed Site Inventory Record.
Except where noted, each box should be filled in with 0=unknown, 1=yes, or 2=no.)

I. GENERAL

1. Site No. |__|__|__|__|__|__|__|__|

2. Site is: |__| (1=vandalized, 2=not vandalized)
   (If vandalized, complete all sections;
   if not vandalized, omit Section III.)

3. Recorded by _____

4. Institution _____

5. Date _____

6. Photo:

   Roll _____

   Exposure(s) _____

II. SITE CHARACTERISTICS

7. Site Type: Architectural |__| Lithic |__| Pottery |__| Cave |__|
   Rockshelter |__| Cist |__| Hearth |__| Rock Art |__| Historic |__|

8. Temporal Period: Paleo-Indian |__| Desert Archaic |__| Basketmaker II-III |__|
   Pueblo I |__| Pueblo II |__| Pueblo III |__| Ute or Navajo |__| Indeterminate |__|

9. Site Size: |__|__|__|__|__|__| sq. m.

III. NATURE OF VANDALISM

10. Location of Disturbance: Room Block |__| Midden |__| Pit Structure |__|
    Cist |__| Burial |__| Rockshelter |__| Rock Wall |__|

11. Method of Disturbance: Shovel |__| Screen |__| Chain |__| Blade |__|
    Backhoe |__| Dynamite |__| Bullets |__| Graffiti |__|

12. Intensity of Disturbance: |__|__|__| % of total site extent

13. Other Evidence of Human Activity:

    Footprints: hiking boot |__| regular |__| cowboy boot |__| other |__| _____
    Fire |__| Cigarette butts |__| brand _____
    Beverage cans and/or pull tops |__| brand _____
    Other garbage |__| _____
    Tire tracks: regular |__| heavy duty (mud, snow) |__| motorcycle |__|
    Mounds of artifacts |__|

IV. SPATIAL CHARACTERISTICS

14. Nearest Road and Rank   Distance: |__|__|__|__| meters
    Rank |__| (1=principal access; 2=all weather; 3=seasonal use; 4=jeep road; 5=trail)

15. Nearest Community and Population Size   Distance: |__|__|__|__| kilometers
    Size |__| (1= <100; 2=101-500; 3=501-1000; 4=1001-5000; 5= >5000)

16. Nearest Intrusion and Type (other than road)   Distance: |__|__|__|__| meters
    Type |__| (1=field; 2=well; 3=reservoir; 4=residence; 5=power line;
    6=chained area; 7=other _____ ; 0=N/A)

V. OTHER   17. Necessity of Site Surveillance |__| 18. Comments: (use back)

APPENDIX C. Specific characteristics of relocated sites.

SITE NO.	PRESENCE OF VANDALISM	SITE CHARACTERISTICS TYPE[1]						PERIOD[2]			ROAD[3]		SPATIAL CHARACTERISTICS COMMUNITY[4]		INTRUSION[5]	
		A	B	C	D	E	F	1	2	3	Distance	Rank	Distance	Size	Distance	Type
5DL6	2	2	1	1	2	2	2	1	2	2	100	4	11.0	3	150	7
5DL8	2	2	2	1	2	1	2	1	2	2	800	4	13.5	3	300	7
5DL14	2	1	1	1	2	2	2	2	1	2	30	4	14.8	3	---	0
5MT102	2	2	1	1	2	2	2	1	2	2	700	3	2.7	1	20	1
5MT137	1	1	1	2	2	2	2	2	2	1	0	4	16.5	1	---	0
5MT145	2	1	1	1	2	2	2	2	2	1	165	4	40.0	1	5160	3
5MT275	1	1	1	1	2	2	2	2	2	2	92	4	28.2	5	100	4
5MT1580	1	1	1	1	2	2	1	1	2	2	250	4	28.4	1	0	6
5MT1595	1	1	1	1	1	2	2	2	2	2	322	4	28.9	1	10	6
5MT1602	1	2	1	1	2	2	2	1	2	2	0	4	23.5	1	10	6
5MT1608	2	1	1	1	2	2	2	2	2	1	161	4	22.6	1	400	6
5MT1618	2	1	1	1	2	2	2	2	2	1	7	5	25.8	1	10	6
5MT1643	1	1	1	1	2	2	2	2	1	2	10	2	16.1	1	3	7
5MT1653	2	1	1	1	2	2	2	2	2	1	500	2	16.0	1	300	1
5MT1667	1	1	1	1	2	2	2	2	2	2	0	4	15.2	5	---	0
5MT1726	2	1	1	2	2	2	2	2	2	1	325	3	26.8	5	---	0
5MT1739	2	1	1	1	2	2	2	2	1	2	225	4	17.1	1	2581	4
5MT1800	2	1	2	2	2	2	2	2	2	1	250	3	28.2	5	300	3
5MT1841	1	1	2	1	2	2	2	2	1	1	100	4	32.6	5	---	0
5MT1850	1	1	1	1	2	2	2	2	2	1	70	4	15.8	5	---	0
5MT1852	1	1	1	1	2	2	2	1	2	2	100	4	16.8	1	2	7
5MT1914	2	1	1	1	2	2	2	2	1	2	20	3	8.0	5	4516	4
5MT1959	2	1	2	1	2	2	2	2	1	2	40	3	10.6	5	---	0
5MT1960	1	1	1	1	2	2	2	2	2	2	25	3	10.5	5	---	0

SITE NO.	PRESENCE OF VANDALISM	SITE CHARACTERISTICS									ROAD[3]	SPATIAL CHARACTERISTICS				
		TYPE[1]						PERIOD[2]				COMMUNITY[4]			INTRUSION[5]	
		A	B	C	D	E	F	1	2	3	Distance	Rank	Distance	Size	Distance	Type
5MT1991	2	2	1	2	2	2	1	1	2	2	100	4	51.3	5	75	7
5MT2014	2	2	1	1	2	2	2	2	1	2	25	3	6.3	5	75	7
5MT2021	1	1	1	1	2	2	2	2	1	2	0	3	4.2	5	645	4
5MT2057	2	1	1	1	2	2	2	2	1	2	5	4	11.1	1	---	0
5MT2058	2	1	1	1	2	2	2	1	2	2	23	4	11.3	1	---	0
5MT2101	2	1	1	1	2	2	2	2	1	2	645	3	15.8	3	250	1
5MT2102	2	1	1	1	2	2	2	2	1	2	645	3	15.8	3	275	1
5MT2107	1	1	1	1	2	2	2	1	2	2	0	4	10.9	1	---	0
5MT2123	1	1	2	1	2	2	2	2	1	2	180	2	10.0	3	50	1
5MT2130	2	2	1	1	2	2	2	2	1	2	644	3	12.9	3	75	1
5MT2131	2	2	1	1	2	2	2	2	1	2	644	3	13.0	3	100	1
5MT2137	1	1	1	1	2	2	2	1	2	2	300	2	7.4	3	0	7
5MT2636	1	1	2	1	2	2	2	1	2	1	645	4	34.0	5	50	7
5MT2637	2	1	1	1	2	2	2	1	2	2	1613	4	34.5	5	---	0
5MT4044	1	1	1	1	2	2	2	2	2	1	200	4	12.1	1	0	6
5MT4068	2	2	1	1	2	2	2	2	2	2	15	4	19.0	1	10	1
5MT4079	2	1	1	1	2	2	2	2	1	2	322	2	16.6	1	500	1
5MT4081	2	1	1	1	2	2	2	2	2	1	322	2	15.8	1	150	1
5MT4082	2	1	1	1	2	2	1	2	1	2	250	2	15.5	1	100	1
5MT4083	2	2	1	1	2	2	2	2	2	1	483	2	15.9	1	400	1
5MT4085	1	1	1	1	2	2	2	2	2	1	484	2	15.5	1	400	1
5MT4087	2	1	1	1	2	2	2	2	2	1	1290	4	28.7	1	4194	4
5MT4090	2	1	1	1	2	2	2	2	2	1	968	4	29.0	1	4194	4
5MT4092	2	1	1	1	2	2	2	2	1	1	1290	4	27.4	1	4516	4

SITE NO.	PRESENCE OF VANDALISM	SITE CHARACTERISTICS TYPE[1]						PERIOD[2]			ROAD[3]		SPATIAL CHARACTERISTICS COMMUNITY[4]		INTRUSION[5]	
		A	B	C	D	E	F	1	2	3	Distance	Rank	Distance	Size	Distance	Type
5MT4095	2	1	1	1	1	2	2	2	2	1	1290	4	27.4	1	4516	4
5MT4282	2	1	2	1	2	2	2	2	1	2	350	4	28.3	1	50	7
5MT4283	2	1	2	1	2	2	2	2	2	1	450	4	27.4	1	50	7
5MT4352	1	1	1	1	2	2	2	2	2	1	130	4	16.1	1	60	7
5MT4355	2	1	1	1	2	2	2	2	2	1	900	4	50.3	5	20	7
5MT4391	2	1	1	1	2	2	2	1	2	2	322	3	31.4	5	---	0
5MT4409	2	1	1	1	2	2	1	1	2	2	700	4	11.3	1	1936	4
5MT4410	2	2	1	1	2	2	1	1	2	2	110	4	11.9	1	2580	4
5MT4575	1	1	1	1	2	2	2	2	2	1	3	4	32.9	1	806	2
5MT4804	2	1	1	1	2	2	2	2	1	2	100	2	22.2	1	50	6
5MT4807	2	1	1	1	2	2	2	2	1	2	500	2	29.4	1	---	0
5MT4808	2	1	1	1	2	2	1	2	1	2	46	3	31.3	1	15	7

[1]Site Type: A=architectural, B=lithic, C=pottery, D=rockshelter, E=hearth, F=cist

[2]Period: 1=Basketmaker III, 2=Pueblo I-Pueblo II, 3=Pueblo II-Pueblo III

[3]Road: distance in meters; rank: 1=principal access, 2=all weather, 3=seasonal use, 4=jeep road, 5=trail

[4]Community: distance in kilometers; size: 1= 100, 2=101-500; 3=501-1000, 4=1001-5000, 5= 5000

[5]Intrusion: distance in meters; type: 1=field, 2=well, 3=reservoir, 4=residence, 5=power line, 6=chained area, 7=other, 0=not applicable

Presence of Vandalism, Site Type, and Period are denoted by 1=yes, 2=no.

161

APPENDIX D. Specific characteristics of relocated Sand Canyon sites.

SITE NO.	PRESENCE OF VANDALISM	PERIOD[1]			ROAD[2]		COMMUNITY[3]		INTRUSION[4]	
		1	2	3	Distance	Rank	Distance	Size	Distance	Type
5MT126	2	2	2	1	323	3	31.3	5	645	2
5MT127	1	2	2	1	323	3	31.0	5	323	2
5MT128	1	1	2	2	161	3	29.4	5	645	2
5MT129	1	2	2	1	15	4	29.7	5	968	2
5MT132	2	2	2	1	323	4	32.6	5	323	2
5MT133	1	2	2	1	485	4	32.9	1	645	4
5MT134	1	2	2	1	485	4	33.2	1	968	2
5MT135	1	2	2	1	322	4	31.6	5	968	2
5MT181	1	2	2	1	5	4	27.1	5	4516	4
5MT185	1	2	2	1	323	3	29.7	5	645	2
5MT186	1	2	2	1	484	4	30.0	1	804	2
5MT256	1	2	2	1	323	3	26.8	1	968	4
5MT257	2	2	1	2	484	3	26.5	1	645	4
5MT258	1	2	1	2	323	3	26.5	1	645	4
5MT261	1	2	2	1	484	3	28.4	5	2581	4
5MT262	1	2	2	1	37	4	27.1	5	1290	4
5MT263	1	2	1	2	92	4	27.5	5	1452	2
5MT264	1	2	2	1	300	4	31.9	5	3548	4
5MT265	1	2	2	1	403	4	32.1	5	3710	4
5MT1803	1	2	2	1	323	3	32.3	5	323	2
5MT1804	2	2	2	1	46	4	32.3	5	323	2
5MT1805	1	2	2	1	30	4	32.1	1	1774	2
5MT1806	1	2	2	1	46	4	32.3	5	1935	2
5MT1807	1	2	2	1	202	4	35.2	5	2903	2

SITE NO.	PRESENCE OF VANDALISM	PERIOD[1] 1	2	3	ROAD[2] Distance	Rank	COMMUNITY[3] Distance	Size	INTRUSION[4] Distance	Type
5MT1808	2	2	2	1	202	4	35.2	5	2903	2
5MT1809	1	2	2	1	202	4	35.2	5	2903	2
5MT1822	1	2	2	1	484	4	35.3	5	3065	2
5MT1823	1	2	2	1	645	4	35.5	5	3226	2
5MT1825	1	2	2	1	161	2	26.8	5	161	4
5MT1826	1	2	2	1	806	4	28.1	1	1290	4
5MT1827	2	2	2	1	645	4	31.0	5	1290	4
5MT1828	1	2	2	1	403	4	30.8	5	1452	4
5MT1829	1	2	2	1	323	4	31.3	5	---	0
5MT1830	2	2	2	1	400	4	31.5	5	---	0
5MT1831	1	2	2	1	300	4	33.2	5	---	0
5MT1841	1	2	2	1	100	4	32.6	5	---	0
5MT1843	2	2	2	1	270	4	33.9	5	---	0
N = 37 All Sites	Yes = 29 (78) No = 8 (22)	1	3	33	Min. 5 Max. 806 X̄ 305	2 = 1 3 = 9 4 =33	Min. 26.5 Max. 35.5 X̄ 31.1	1 = 8 5 =29	Min. 161 Max. 4516 X̄ 1557	0 = 5 2 =18 4 =14
N = 29 Vandalized Sites Only		1	2	36	Min. 5 Max. 806 X̄ 296	2 = 1 3 = 7 4 =21	Min. 26.5 Max. 35.5 X̄ 30.9	1 = 7 5 =22	Min. 161 Max. 4516 X̄ 1681	0 = 3 2 =14 4 =12

Unless otherwise specified, 1=yes and 2=no.

[1]Period: 1=BMIII, 2=PI-PII, 3=PII-PIII.

[2]Road: distance in meters; rank: 2=all weather, 3=seasonal use, 4=jeep road

[3]Community: distance in kilometers; size: 1= <100, 5= > 5000

[4]Intrusion: distance in meters; type: 0=not applicable, 2=well, 4=residence

APPENDIX E

INFORMANT QUESTIONNAIRE

The text of the questionnaire is presented below. Since it was originally designed to be filled out by respondents, a definition and introductory comment was included on page 1.

Modifications

Question 16: The second part of the question, "activities you participate in most regularly," was cumbersome and confusing and was deleted.

Question 17: Since everyone had a collection, the "If NO" section was not pertinent. Some informants did know of people who made sherd collages.

Question 75: Differentiation of going to a site and digging at a site was difficult, since many people in the sample did not dig. The question was rephrased so that the #2 part was only asked of those who dug, or was asked to solicit answers about friends or acquaintances who dig.

Question 76: Respondents were asked to name all places that were good for collecting or digging, and responses were tallied by frequency rather than rated by 1st, 2nd, 3rd choice.

Question 81 was modified to include the question, "What did you do with the bones?"

Complete text of comments to open-ended questions was not included in the text and has not been included in appendices because it frequently tends to be repetitive. Relevant quotes have been extracted.

165

QUESTIONNAIRE

NOTE: An "artifact" is any man-made object, but refers here to such items as arrowheads, potsherds and pots, historic bottles and other objects found at prehistoric or historic sites.

PLEASE ANSWER ALL QUESTIONS. We would also very much appreciate your comments.

1. Your sex: Male _____ ; Female _____ .

2. Are you married? Yes _____ No _____ .

3. Number of children _____ , Ages of oldest _____ and youngest _____ .

4. How long have you lived in southwestern Colorado? _____ years.

5. If you were born in southwestern Colorado, when did your parents move to the area? _____

6. Your occupation? _____

7. Do you live in town? _____ That town is _____
   or out of town? _____ Your nearest town is _____ ; miles _____ .

8. Do you belong to any local clubs or organizations? Yes _____ No _____ .
   If yes, please list _____

9. Have you ever held a public office? Yes _____ No _____ .

10. Please check activities you regularly participate in:
    Recreational 4-wheeldriving _____ ; Camping _____ ; Hunting _____ ; Fishing _____ ;
    Picnicking _____ ; Boating _____ ; Rockhounding _____ .

11. Are you interested in local archaeology? Yes _____ No _____ .

12. Are you interested in local history? Yes _____ No _____ .

13. Have you read any books on archaeology or local history? Yes _____ No _____ .

14. Have you visited any of the following places. (Please indicate those you have visited)
    Mesa Verde _____ ; Hovenweep _____ ; Escalante Ruin _____ ; Lowry Ruins _____ ;
    Other Southwest ruins _____ ; San Juan mining ghost towns, such as Camp Bird, Illium _____ .

15. Have you visited the current Dolores Project dig that is open to the public?
    Yes _____ No _____ .

16. Please check Column #1 for any activities you have ever participated in. Please check Column #2 for those activities in which you participate most regularly.

    #1   #2
    ___ ___ Collecting prehistoric artifacts (such as arrowheads) from the surface of the ground;
    ___ ___ Digging for prehistoric artifacts;
    ___ ___ Collecting historic artifacts (such as bottles) from the surface of the ground;
    ___ ___ Digging for historic artifacts;
    ___ ___ Moving Indian ruin rubble (such as clearing agricultural land);
    ___ ___ Removing parts of structures (such as obtaining barnwood or firewood).

17. Do you have a personal collection of artifacts? Yes _____ No _____ .
    If NO, what do you do with the artifacts you find? (Indicate as many as are applicable.) Leave them on the ground _____ ; Sell them _____ ; Use them for making items (such as sherd collages, arrowhead coffee tables, etc.) that you: Keep _____ ; Give as gifts _____ ; Sell _____ .
    Other: _____

page 1

If you do have a collection, what do you collect? Whole pots____;
Potsherds____; Arrowheads____; Other stone tools, such as____; Other, such as____.
Bottles____; Miscellaneous historic items____.

What is the best piece in your collection? (Please describe specifically.)

What item(s) would you consider to be "first rate" find? (Describe specifically.)

How many items are in your collection?
Do you place a dollar value on it? Yes____ No____ Amount $____.
Does it consist completely of found items? Yes____ No____, or do you:
Trade for items____; Buy items____; Other means of acquiring
How:

Do you display your collection? Yes____ No____.
In your home?____. If not in your home, where?____.
Have you ever donated any part of your collection to a museum? Yes____ No____.
IF YES, where?

18. Have you ever sold any artifacts you found? Yes____ No____.
IF YES, of what did they consist? Pottery____; Arrowheads____; Bottles____; or
Other:
Did you sell to a Local individual____; A local store that sells artifacts____;
Someone out of town (from____); Someone out of state (from____).

19. Would the sale of your artifacts increase your interest in artifact hunting?
Yes____ No____.

20. Do you know others who have sold artifacts? Yes____ No____.
How many do you know? 1-2____; 3-5____; 6-10____; Over 10____.
How many sell regularly? 1-2____; 3-5____; 6-10____; Over 10____.
Do they sell to: Local buyers____; Out of town buyers____; Out of state buyers____.

21. What items do you think sell best? (Please be as specific as possible.)

22. Do you specifically look for certain objects to sell? Yes____ No____.
23. Do you know people who buy and resell prehistoric artifacts? Yes____ No____.
24. Is it difficult to find a buyer? Yes____ No____.
25. Do you know any professional archaeologists? Yes____ No____.
26. Have you talked to any lately? Yes____ No____.
27. In your opinion, what do archaeologists do?

Do you think an archaeologist's work is different from what others do when they
hunt or dig for objects? Yes____ No____. If YES, explain differences:

28. Do you feel that the archaeological portion of the Dolores Project is
justified? Yes____ No____.
Do local people know enough about it? Yes____ No____.
Have local people been involved enough? Yes____ No____.

29. Has the large number of archaeologists associated with the Dolores Project
changed the community in any way? Yes____ No____. IF YES, in what way:

30. Have you ever seen or talked with the Dolores Project archaeologists? Yes____ No____.
Have the Dolores Project archaeologists done anything for the community?
Yes____ No____.
Are these archaeologists typical of archaeologists in general? Yes____ No____.
Are they similar to archaeologists at Mesa Verde? Yes____ No____.
Are they similar to archaeologists from other Federal agencies? Yes____ No____.
Is there a difference between government archaeologists and archaeologists who
work for universities or private companies? Yes____ No____. IF YES, please
describe differences:

31. Is it important to you that objects from sites stay in the area? Yes____ No____.
32. Do you feel that archaeologists have removed much from the area? Yes____ No____.
33. Do you feel that local artifact hunters and collectors have removed much from
the area by selling or otherwise moving of collections? Yes____ No____.

34. Would you be interested in participating in a local organization of amateur
archaeologists? Yes____ No____.

35. Do you feel that most people who hunt for artifacts are primarily:
Locals____, or Tourists____.

36. Does the government have the right to tell you not to dig or collect on
public lands? Yes____ No____.

37. Do you think that different government agencies (BLM, Forest Service, Park
Service, Bureau of Reclamation) have the same attitude about artifact hunters?
Yes____ No____. IF NO, how are they different?

38. Do you know what the term "Cultural Resources" means? Yes____ No____.
IF YES, please define briefly:

39. Is artifact hunting or digging for artifacts a family activity? Yes____ No____.
40. If you hunt or dig for artifacts, did you first become involved in these
activities through: Your parents as a child____; Your friends as a child____;
Your own interest____; Others as an adult____.

41. Is this a personal hobby? Yes____ No____.
42. When did you first dig or hunt for artifacts? 0-5 years ago____;
6-20 years ago____; Over 20 years ago____.

43. How often? ____ times per year; ____ times per month.
44. When was the last time? This week____; This month____; Within past six
months____; Within past 12 months____; Over a year ago____.

45. Have your parents, or older family members, done this? Yes____ No____.
46. Do your friends do this? Yes____ No____.

47. If you have children, do they do this? Yes _____ No _____.

48. Of the people you know, how many do this? None _____; A few _____; A half _____ Most _____; All _____. Are these people mostly: Male _____ or Female _____.

49. Of those people in Question 48, what are age ranges primarily? Under 14 _____; 14-21 _____; 22-29 _____; Over 30 _____.

50. Do you regard artifact hunting, or digging for artifacts, as a local tradition? Yes _____ No _____.

51. Do you think you are typical as compared to others who engage in these activities? Yes _____ No _____. If NO, please list your differences:

52. Do you hunt or dig for artifacts: Alone _____; With 1-2 others _____; With 3-4 others _____; With more than 4 others _____.

53. What is the average time spent when you are doing these activities? 2 hours or less _____; One-half day _____; 1 day _____; 2 or more days _____.

54. When do you do these activities most often? On weekdays _____; Weekends _____; Holidays _____.

55. What time of day? Morning _____; Afternoon _____; Evening _____; Night _____; Varies from trip to trip _____.

56. In what season do you most frequently do these activities? Spring _____; Summer _____; Fall _____; Winter _____.

57. Do occupational responsibilities (such as farm work) make a difference as to when you go? Yes _____ No _____.

58. How far ahead of time do you plan your trips? No planning _____; Less than 1 day _____; 1-2 days _____; 3-7 days _____; More than 7 days _____.

59. Do you return to the same place several times? Yes _____ No _____. If NO, do you always go to a different place? Yes _____ No _____.

60. How do you decide where to go? (Indicate as many as applicable.) Easy place to get to _____; Found objects at location previously _____; Heard location was good _____ from: Friends _____; Family _____; Others: (Who?) _____.

61. Site is a traditional place to look _____; Site is remote and untouched _____. Considering all the locations you have visited, would you estimate these locations are: Within 2 miles of each other _____; 3-5 miles apart _____; 6-10 miles apart _____; 11-20 miles apart _____; More than 20 miles apart _____.

62. What are your favorite places to look for artifacts?

63. Do you have sites on your own property? Yes _____ No _____.

64. What is the usual distance you drive to get to a site? 0-5 miles _____; 6-10 miles _____; 11-20 miles _____; Over 20 miles _____.

65. What is the farthest distance you have driven to a site? _____ miles.

66. How far do you usually walk to get to a site? 0-100 yards _____; 100 yards to 1/4 mile _____; 1/4 to 1/2 mile _____; 1/2-1 mile _____; Over 1 mile _____.

67. What is the farthest distance you have walked to a site? _____ (Yards) or (Miles) _____.

68. What types of roads do you drive on most frequently to get to a site? Paved _____; Maintained dirt _____; 4-wheel drive _____; Oil/gas drilling access roads _____; Agricultural access roads (such as through bean or wheat fields) _____; Drive off roads _____.

69. What vehicle do you usually use to get there? 2-wheel drive car _____; 2-wheel drive truck _____; 4-wheel drive vehicle _____.

70. Have you ever used motorcycles in these activities? Yes _____ No _____.

71. Have you ever gone to sites in or near chained areas? Yes _____ No _____. Do you prefer these sites? Yes _____ No _____.

72. Have you ever gone to sites in or near agricultural areas (such as sites in bean or wheat fields)? Yes _____ No _____. Do you prefer these sites? Yes _____ No _____.

73. Are sites you go to easy to see and identify? Yes _____ No _____. Do they stand out because of: Thicker vegetation _____; Lack of vegetation _____; Location in caves or alcoves _____.

74. What is the land status of the areas you usually go to? Private _____; Public _____; My own land _____; Don't know _____.

75. Please check in Column #1 the kinds of places you go to most often. Check in Column #2 kinds of places you have dug at.

#1	#2	
_____	_____	Large number of artifacts on the ground but no structures;
_____	_____	Large rubble mounds;
_____	_____	Small rubble mounds;
_____	_____	Stone structures (such as rooms, towers);
_____	_____	Cliff dwellings;
_____	_____	Rock art;
_____	_____	Homesteads;
_____	_____	Railroad-related structures;
_____	_____	Mining related structures;
_____	_____	Dugouts;
_____	_____	Historic trash pile with no structures.

76. Once you are at a site, where is the best place to collect or dig? (List preference by numbering (1st, 2nd, 3rd choice places) Trash area _____; Rooms _____; Depressions _____; Close to cliff face _____; Near Large rocks _____; Other: _____.

77. If you dig at sites, what tools do you use? Shovels _____; Screens _____; Trowels _____; Rakes _____; Tractors, backhoes, or other power equipment _____; Other: _____.

78. How much time do you spend digging? 0-2 hours _____; 3-4 hours _____; 5-8 hours _____; Over 8 hours _____.

79. What have you found digging? Whole pots _____; Potsherds _____; Arrowheads _____; Pendants or jewelry _____; Other: _____.

80. Is it best to dig: A few large holes _____ OR Several small holes _____.

81. Have you ever found a burial? Yes _____ No _____. If YES, did you collect: Bones _____; Artifacts _____; Both bones and artifacts _____; Made no collection _____.

82. Are you looking for burials? Yes _____ No _____.

83. Is it better to go to a site that: (Check all that are appropriate) Has already been dug into _____; Has not already been dug into _____; Has eroded naturally _____; Is locally well-known _____; Has a large number of artifacts on the ground surface _____.

84. How many rock art sites do you know of locally? None____; 1-2____; 3-4____; 5 or more____;
Have any of these sites been defaced or written over? Yes____ No____
Have any of these sites been shot at? Yes____ No____

85. Is it wrong to sign your name or write something else at:
a) A rock art site   Yes____ No____
b) A ruin   Yes____ No____
c) Cabin or other historic site   Yes____ No____

86. Can you tell how old a site is? Yes____ No____, If YES, how do you determine the age of the site? Please explain.
_____

Do you prefer to go to sites of a certain age? Yes____ No____.
If YES, what age? _____

87. Are you aware that collecting and digging on public lands are illegal? Yes____ No____. Do you know anything about the legislation that makes it illegal and when it was enacted? Yes____ No____. Do others you know who dig or collect know? Yes____ No____

88. Have you ever seen a sign post saying that collecting or digging on public lands was illegal? Yes____ No____. Do you think most local people who dig or collect know? Yes____ No____. Did this discourage you? Yes____ No____
Did this make you aware of ruins you previously did not know about? Yes____ No____

89. Have you ever seen any BLM personnel out on patrol? Yes____ No____
Have you ever talked to any BLM personnel on patrol? Yes____ No____

90. Do you think that fences or other physical barriers keep artifact hunters away from ruins? Yes____ No____

91. Do you think that closing roads and trails keeps people away? Yes____ No____

92. How widespread is digging and collecting in this part of the state? (Please check one.)
Everyone does it____; Most people do it____;
About half the people do it____; A few people do it____;
A small minority of people do it____

93. Have you ever heard of anyone being convicted, fined or jailed for artifact hunting on public lands? Yes____ No____. If YES, where did this incident happen?
_____
When did it happen? _____
Have you ever heard about anyone in southwestern Colorado being convicted on this charge? Yes____
Do you feel that such news would act as a deterrent to artifact hunting? Yes____ No____

94. Have you ever heard any radio or television programs, or announcements telling people not to hunt or dig for artifacts or stressing the importance of preserving "cultural resources?" Yes____ No____
Have you ever seen any local newspaper articles on this subject? Yes____ No____
Have you ever heard of anyone giving a talk locally on this subject? Yes____ No____
Is this message taught in school locally? Yes____ No____

95. Do you have any ideas or opinions about how the government should manage Indian ruins, historic cabins, and the other places discussed above?
Yes____ No____. If YES, please comment: _____

96. Please check the attitude closest to your own:
All these sites should be protected in some way.
____ Most of these sites should be protected in some way.
____ A few significant sites should be protected in some way.
____ There are so many sites that the ones already protected are sufficient.

If you feel that any sites should be protected, how should this be done?
_____

Responses to Questions 95 and 96 of the Questionnaire.

Question 95.   Do you have any ideas or opinions about how the government should manage Indian ruins, historic cabins, and the other places discussed above?

Questionnaire #   Response

1.   The government should enforce heavier fines, and arrests and convictions should be easier. Now, a pothunter with a sack full of pots can't even be arrested.

2.   The government should help the living instead of the dead. Sites should be left buried. A certain amount of exploration is all right, but digs should not be financed.

3.   My biggest gripe is that BLM is trying to get too close to the private land owner, to say too much about what he can and cannot do. The government should not tell farmers what to do with ruins.

   BLM should have started 40 or 50 years ago because the ruins are really messed up already. But there's still a lot to preserve. BLM has been at fault through not enforcing the law. I think sites should be excavated and preserved and there should be a big public park like Mesa Verde here, so things can be kept in the area.

4.   No comment.

5.   The government should pick out the best ruins and stabilize them. Little campsites are not worth preserving. Money should be spent on stabilization, not excavation. There are some beautiful ruins still left, but they are deteriorating rapidly.

6.   Not every rock pile through the trees should be protected. The big sites should be looked after.

7.   What BLM should do to manage their ruins has a lot to do with their tactics. They have to approach people on their level; they have to understand what is going on and they have to persuade people. They must not call people vandals, thieves, and pothunters without cause.

   Also, they should hire locals to work with local people, not Easterners. They should stop telling people what to do.

   There's been some publicity on their increased fines. This is stopping people who were involved as a hobby, but not the professionals. The illegality doubles the prices the professionals can get. There's a great increase in the market as a result. Once a piece is on the market the knowledge is gone. Instead of trying to stop the sale, BLM should be interviewing people and recovering the knowledge.

There is more local knowledge than BLM seems to realize and this is a cultural resource that will soon be lost as old-timers die. Local people are willing to work with archaeologists but feel they have to hide what they know and have done. Their knowledge is therefore destroyed. It's bad publicity to call junk the artifacts people dug up 50 years ago and have been proud of.

8. Some fine examples of sites should be chosen and preserved. It's crazy to stop development because of one piece of pottery on the road. There's pottery everywhere. All the sites should not be preserved.

9. I don't have any ideas except for them to continue their present policy. Maybe some sites should have roofs. Wind, sun, and time changes them.

10. I have no opinions. The problem is that I don't want the government to have the personnel or the power to close ruins or roads. Education is the best way. The message to get across is "Once this is gone, there is no more." A few easy-to-get-to sites should be developed with self-guided tours, and this message should be incorporated.

11. The government can afford to open a few sites for exhibit and protect the rest. Limited government funding is a problem. The extensive area makes management a near impossible task. This is a problem even with patrol.

12. The land is so scattered. It's hard to administer and protect. Too much manpower would be needed for adequate protection. BLM is flying patrols now. We can't see how they can do better.

13. We've known about the Antiquities Law for a long time. It was passed in 1906. The law should have been enforced from when it was first passed. With the Wetherill brothers and such; there was large scale potting back in those days.

14. Patrol is not the way. Scaring people is not the way. Getting people more interested and educated is the way. Also, the government should prevent the sale of artifacts, while encouraging the public display of local collections. The Dove Creek Bank collection is a good example--it has the owner's name on it.

Also, the government should go around and talk to people about their collections. A local museum with people's names on their collections would be a good idea. These people have put in a lot of effort in artifact hunting. It's a ripoff for the government to confiscate collections. Collections are often a source of local, individual, and family pride, only to be sold in very hard times. With this talk about the government confiscating collections, people are being riled up with no cause against archaeologists and environmentalists.

Archaeology fees hurt the small businessman.

15. The government should continue to leave private property ownership untouched. Law enforcement efforts should be directed at very rich areas that are worth restoration or excavation. Less important areas should be made less accessible (for example, energy companies should be told to block roads after use, and the "no motorized vehicle" areas should be expanded and enforced).

16. The government should keep out.

17. Everybody has a different opinion about what the government should do.

18. The ruins should be protected to a certain extent.

19. No comment.

20. No comment.

Question 96.   If you feel that <u>any</u> sites should be protected, how should this be done?

<u>Questionnaire #</u>   <u>Response</u>

1. So few sites are of any value any more anyway. All the history can be obtained from half a dozen sites. 90% of it can be obtained from one site. The ruins in the fields have been destroyed and it's the same with the ones on BLM land.

2. Mesa Verde is a supreme example of sites being protected as they should be. The Escalante Ruin is open to the public with no supervision. It could be vandalized. Also, natural deterioration should be prevented.

3. More sites should be excavated. Also, although high penalties are the biggest deterrent to pothunting, more control of the market means higher prices for illegal pots and that makes the market problem worse.

   It bothers me that I know more than many archaeologists. I know that vessels have been broken on the Dolores Project through carelessness in excavating. I hear through word of mouth that the archaeologists here know they don't have the experience.

4. The sites designated to be protected should be <u>well</u> protected and money and energy should be spent to make sure <u>this</u> is done.

5. Stabilization should be stressed above all other forms of protection.

7. Most sites should be protected where there is a possibility of gaining knowledge.

   Site protection is being carried too far when drill rigs are being moved for no reason. People who work in energy development see

right through it. Archaeologists are abusing energy development--
the people sent out to do the clearances need to be more knowledgeable. The costs to the oil companies are substantial. If
they weren't being cheated on, energy people would be happy to
work with archaeologists.

Another source of friction is that archaeologists are doing the same
thing as pothunters. We won't see any Dolores Project write-up for
years and years. Archaeologists are just digging things up legally.
People need to see the Dolores Project artifacts <u>now</u>. They need to
see that the project is really worthwhile. Only the state representa-
tives and the other officials are shown the vessels--the public is
not welcome to see them. Archaeologists promote a separatist attitude. They feel they are being challenged by local people. These
projects should be let out to companies and run on a more professional
level. There's been a lot of government propaganda. Also, despite
the income the project has brought in, there's been a sort of local
public versus transient archaeologists attitude.

BLM will never stop the digging on public lands. They should be
spending their money on gathering information, which is the whole
purpose of not destroying the ruins. They're 20 years too late in
their approach. Now, there's more natural than human destruction.
The big pothunting happened up through the 60's. There are still a
lot of pothunters out there, but they're hard to get at.

If BLM makes it illegal to possess pots, people will destroy what
they have. They'll break all their pieces.

8. 80% of the sites can be written off. There are hundreds and
    thousands of sites in this area. You have to keep in mind that
    people must make a living off this country.

    The government should make a small park to protect these few sig-
    nificant sites, like Hovenweep for example. The destruction has
    already been done and there are very few commercial pothunters
    out there (Utah is worse--there are a lot of diggers over there).
    The government should make a picnic place for people, but the ruins
    don't need to be dug. What would people look at with no unexcavated
    ruins?

    There should be a reward for catching vandals, for example, same as
    a bounty for people caught destroying signs.

    The oil companies must be regulated to control their greed. Although
    road builders and such usually go around ruins because it's easier,
    there is a little bit of related digging and collecting.

    Much feeling about excessive government control is unwarranted.

    The ruins are mostly <u>not</u> destroyed, just potted some. But pothunting
    is declining steadily, by 500% for the amount of people who live here
    now. It's practically nil. As a young person, I was admired for
    finding pots. Now, it's like smoking. You're considered a dirty
    bird if you do it. Public opinion frowns on digging on public land.
    It used to be that nobody would turn you in. Now, they would.

9. There's nothing worth saving at the minor sites.

10. See comments from question 95.

11. Although I feel all the sites should somehow be protected, I don't know any way to do it. The youth programs (YACC) are a good means of getting the message across to local kids.

12. See comments from question 95. The government does not have the right to tell private people what to do about ruins on private lands.

14. Nobody should be allowed to dig the protected sites, including archaeologists. Undug sites need to be left for future generations.

15. Limit visitation and don't advertise the sites.

16. The sites should be protected same as now--just the big ones.

17. It's nice to preserve lands but you can't preserve everything.

18. I don't know.

19. No comment.

20. No comment.